# Tamerlane by Nicholas Rowe

**A TRAGEDY.**

**As it is Acted at the New Theatre in Little Lincolns Inn Fields. By Her Majesty's Servants.**

Nicholas Rowe was born in Little Barford, Bedfordshire, England, on June 20th, 1674.

He was educated at Highgate School, and then at Westminster School under the tutelage of Dr. Busby.

In 1688, Rowe became a King's Scholar, and then in 1691 gained entrance into Middle Temple. This was his father's decision (he was a barrister) who felt that his son had made sufficient progress to study law. While at Middle Temple, he decided that studying law was easier if seen as a system of rational government and impartial justice and not as a series of precedents, or collection of positive precepts.

On his father's death, when he was nineteen, he became the master of a large estate and an independent fortune. His future path now was to ignore law and write poetry with a view to eventually writing plays.

The Ambitious Stepmother, Rowe's first play, produced in 1700 at Lincoln's Inn Fields by Thomas Betterton and set in Persepolis, was well received.

This was followed in 1701 by Tamerlane. In this play the conqueror Timur represented William III, and Louis XIV is denounced as Bajazet. It was for many years regularly acted on the anniversary of William's landing at Torbay.

The Fair Penitent (1703), an adaptation of Massinger and Field's The Fatal Dowry, was pronounced by Dr Johnson as one of the most pleasing tragedies ever written in English. He noted that, "The story is domestic, and therefore easily received by the imagination, and assimilated to common life; the diction is exquisitely harmonious, and soft or spritely as occasion requires."

In 1704, he tried his hand at comedy, with The Biter at Lincoln's Inn Fields. The play is said to have amused no one except the author, and Rowe returned to tragedy in Ulysses (1706). For Johnson, this play was to share the fate of many such plays based on mythological heroes, as, "We have been too early acquainted with the poetical heroes to expect any pleasure from their revival"

The Royal Convert (1707) dealt with the persecutions endured by Aribert, son of Hengist and the Christian maiden Ethelinda. The story was set in England in an obscure and barbarous age. Rodogune was a tragic character, of high spirit and violent passions, yet with a wicked with a soul that would have been heroic if it had been virtuous.

Rowe is however well known for his work on Shakespeare's plays. He published the first 18th century edition of Shakespeare in six volumes in 1709. His practical knowledge of the stage helped him divide the plays into scenes and acts, with entrances and exits of the players noted. The spelling of names was normalized and each play prefixed with a dramatis personae. This 1709 edition was also the first to be illustrated, a frontispiece engraving being provided for each play. Unfortunately, Rowe based his text on the discredited Fourth Folio, a failing which many succeeding him also followed.

Rowe also wrote a short biography of William Shakespeare, entitled, Some Account of the Life of Mr. William Shakespear.

For two years (1709-11) he acted as under-secretary to the Duke of Queensberry when he was principal secretary of state for Scotland.

In Dublin in 1712 a revival of his earlier play, Tamerlane, at a time when political passions were running high, the performance provoked a serious riot.

The Tragedy of Jane Shore, played at Drury Lane with Mrs Oldfield in the title role in 1714. It ran for nineteen nights, and kept the stage longer than any other of Rowe's works. In the play, which consists chiefly of domestic scenes and private distress, the wife is forgiven because she repents, and the husband is honoured because he forgives.

The Tragedy of Lady Jane Grey followed in 1715, and as this play was not successful, it was his last foray into the medium.

Whilst his plays met with little success at the time his poems were received extremely well. Although he was not prolific nor his output large the quality was high.

With the accession to the throne of George I he was made a surveyor of customs, and then, in 1715, he succeeded Nahum Tate as poet laureate.  It was the high point of his artistic life.

He was also appointed clerk of the council to the Prince of Wales, and in 1718 was nominated by Lord Chancellor Parker as clerk of the presentations in Chancery.

Nicholas Rowe died on December 6th, 1718, and was buried in Westminster Abbey.

Rowe married first a daughter of a Mr Parsons and left a son John. By his second wife Anne, née Devenish, he had a daughter Charlotte.


## Index of Contents

Publishers Note

Unfortunately over the past 300 years some words on several lines of the following play have been lost. These are indicated by [.....] where that occasionally happens.


TO THE RIGHT HONOURABLE WILLIAM, LORD MARQUISS OF HARTINGTON

My LORD,

Every body is now so full of Business, that things of this kind, which are generally taken for the Entertainment of leisure Hours only, look like Impertinence and Interruption. I am sure it is a Reason why I ought to beg your Lordship's Pardon, for troubling you with this Tragedy; Not but that Poetry has always been, and will still be the Entertainment of all wise Men, that have any Delicacy in their Knowledge; Yet at so Critical a Juncture as this is, I must confess I think your Lordship ought to give intirely into those Publick Affairs, which at this time seem to Demand you. It is that happy Turn which your Lordship has to Business, that right Understanding of your Country's Interest, and that constant Zeal to pursue it, that just Thinking, that strong and persuasive Elocution, that firm and generous Resolution, which upon all Occasions you have shewn in Parliaments; and to add, that which is the crowning good Quality, your Lordship's continual Adherence and Unshaken Loyalty to His present Majesty, which make you at this time so necessary to the Publick. I must confess, (tho' there is no part in your Lordship's Character, but what the World should be fond of) I cannot help Distinguishing the last Instance very particularly: It is doing (methinks) such a Justice to Goodness, to Greatness, and to Right Reason, that Posterity will believe there could be no Man of good Sense, but what must have agreed with your Lordship in it. When the next Age shall Read the History of this, What Excuse can they make for those who did not Admire a Prince whose Life has been a Series of good Offices done to Mankind? When they shall reckon up his Labours from the Battle of Seneff, to some Glorious Action, which shall be his Last, (and which I therefore hope is very far remov'd from the Present Time?) Will they ever believe that he could have been too well lov'd, or too faithfully serv'd and defended? The Great Things which he did before we had that immediate Interest in him, which we now happily have, is a noble and just Subject for Panegyrick; but as Benefits done to Others, can never touch us so sensibly as those we receive our selves, tho' the Actions may be equally great; so, methinks, I can hardly have patience to run back to his having sav'd his own Country, when I consider he has since done the same for Us; Let that be sufficient to Us, for all we can say of him or do for him. What Dangers and Difficulties has he not struggled through, for the Honour and Safety of these Kingdoms? 'Tis a common Praise, and what every one speaks, to say, He has continually expos'd his Life for his People; But there are some things more particular in his Character, some things rarely found amongst the Policies of Princes; a Zeal for Religion, moderated by Reason, without the Rage and Fire of Persecution; a charitable Compassion for those who cannot be convinc'd, and an unalterable Perseverance in those Principles of whose Truth he is satisfy'd; a desire of War for the sake of Peace; and of Peace for the Good and Honour of his Subjects equally with his own; a pious Care for composing Factions, tho' to foment them might make him Arbitrary; and a generous Ambition that only aims at Pow'r, to enable him to do good to all the rest of the World. I might add here, that Inviolable and Religious Observance of his Royal Word, which the best part of the Pow'rs of Europe, have so frequently and so happily, for themselves, depended upon in the greatest Emergencies. But as this Virtue is generally reckon'd as no more than that common Honesty, which the meanest Man would blush to be without, so it can hardly claim a Place amongst the more particular Excellencies of a Great Prince. It were to be wish'd, indeed, that the World were honest to such a degree, and that there were not that scandalous defect of common Morality. Certainly nothing can be more shocking to Humanity, to the Peace and Order of the World; nothing can approach nearer to that Savage state of Nature, in which every Man is to eat his fellow if he can master him, than an avow'd Liberty of breaking thro' all the most solemn Engagements of publick Faith. 'Tis something that brands a Man with an Infamy, which nothing can extenuate or wipe out; he may protest and pretend to explain his meaning, but the World has generally too much indignation for the Affront, to bear it at that easie rate. Ministers and Secretaries of State, may display their own Parts in Memorials, with as much Pomp and Flourish as they please: I fancy the common answer upon such Occasions will always be, You have deceiv'd us grosly, and we neither can nor will trust you any more. When this Vice comes amongst Men of the first Rank, it is the more shocking, and I could wish there were none such, to whose charge it might be laid.

Some People (who do me a very great Honour in it) have fancy'd, that in the Person of Tamerlane I have alluded to the greatest Character of the present Age, I don't know, whether I ought not to apprehend a great deal of Danger from avowing a Design like that. It may be a Task indeed worthy the greatest Genius, which this, or any other Time has produc'd: But therefore I ought not to stand the shock of a Parallel, least it should be seen, to my Disadvantage, how far the Hero has transcended the Poet's Thought. There are many Features, 'tis true, in that Great Man's Life, not unlike His Majesty: His Courage, his Piety, his Moderation, his Justice, and his Fatherly Love of his People, but above all, his Hate of Tyranny and Oppression, and his zea lous Care for the Common Good of Mankind, ⟨◊⟩ large Resemblance of Him: Several Incidents are alike in their Stories; and there wants nothing to his Majesty but such a deciding Victory, as that by which Tamerlane gave Peace to the World. That is yet to come: But I hope we may reasonably expect it from the unanimity of the present Parliament, and so formidable a Force as that Unanimity will give Life and Vigour to.

If your Lordship can find any thing in this Poem like a Prince, who is so justly the Object of your Lordship's, and indeed of the World's Veneration, I persuade my self it will prevail with you to forgive every thing else that you find amiss. You will excuse the Faults in Writing, for the goodness of the Intention. I hope too, your Lordship will not be displeas'd, that I take this opportunity of renewing the Honour which I formerly had, to be known to your Lordship, and which gives me at once the Pleasure of expressing those Just and Dutiful Sentiments I have for his Majesty, and that strong Inclination which I have always had to be thought,

My Lord,

Your Lordships most Obedient,
Humble Servant,
N. ROWE

MEN

Tamerlane

Bajazet, Emperor of the Turks

Axalla, an Italian Prince, General and Favourite of Tamerlane

Moneses, a Grecian Prince, and a Christian

Stratocles, his Friend

Prince of Tanais, Kinsman and General to Tamerlane

Omar, a Tartar General

Mirvan, Parthian General to Tamerlane

Zama, Parthian General to Tamerlane

Haly, Favourite Eunuch to Bajazet

A Turkish Dervise

WOMEN

Arpasia, a Grecian Princess

Selima, Daughter of Bajazet


Parthian and Tartar Soldiers

Mutes belonging to Bajazet

Other Attendants


SCENE: Tamerlane's Camp, near Angoria in Galatia.


PROLOGUE

Spoke by **MR BETTERTON**.

Of all the Muses various Labours, none
Have lasted longer, or have higher flown,
Than those that tell the Fame by ancient Hero's won.
With Pleasure, Rome and Great Augustus, heard
Arms and the Man sung by the Mantuan Bard;
In spight of Time, the sacred Story lives,
And Caesar and his Empire still survives.
Like him, (tho' much unequal to his Flame)
Our Author makes a pious Prince his Theme,
High with the foremost Names in Arms he stood,
Had fought, and suffer'd for his Country's Good,
Yet sought not Fame, but Peace, in Fields of Blood.
Safe under him his happy People sate,
And griev'd at distance for their Neighbours Fate.

Whilst with Success, a Turkish Monarch Crown'd,
Like spreading Flame, deform'd the Nations round:
With Sword and Fire he forc'd his impious way
To Lawless Pow'r, and Universal Sway:
Some abject States for fear the Tyrant join;
Others for Gold their Liberties resign,
And venal Princes sold their Right Divine.
'Till Heav'n, the growing Evil to redress,
Sent Tamerlane to give the World a Peace.
The Hero rouz'd, asserts the Glorious Cause,
And to the Field the chearful Soldier draws:
Around in Crowds his valiant Leaders wait,
Anxious for Glory, and secure of Fate;
Well pleas'd, once more to venture on his side,
And prove that Faith again, which had so oft been betray'd.
The peaceful Fathers, who in Senates meet,
Approve an Enterprize so Just, so Great;
While with their Prince's Arms, their Voice thus join'd,
Gains half the Praise of having sav'd Mankind.
Ev'n in a Circle, where, like this, the Fair
Were met, the bright Assembly did declare,
Their House with one consent were for the War.
Each urg'd her Lover to unsheath his Sword,
And never spare a Man who broke his Word.
Thus fir'd, the Brave on to the Danger press;
Their Arms were crown'd abroad, with just Success,
And blest at Home with Beauty and with Peace.


TAMERLANE

ACT I

SCENE I

SCENE Before Tamerlane's Tent

Enter the **PRINCE of TANAIS**, **ZAMA** and **MIRVAN**.

**PRINCE of TANAIS**
Hail to the Sun! from whose returning Light
The chearful Soldier's Arms new Lustre take,
To deck the Pomp of Battle; Oh, my Friends!
Was ever such a glorious Face of War?
See, from this height! how all Galatia's Plains
With Nations numberless are cover'd o'er;
Who like a Deluge, hide the Face of Earth,

And leave no Object, in the vast Horizon,
But glitt'ring Arms, and Skies.

**ZAMA**
Our Asian World
From this important Day expects a Lord,
This day they hope an end of all their Woes,
Of Tyranny, of Bondage, and Oppression
From our Victorious Emp'ror, Tamerlane.

**MIRVAN**
Well has our Holy Alha mark'd him out
The Scourge of lawless Pride, and dire Ambition,
The great Avenger of the groaning World.
Well has he worn the sacred Cause of Justice
Upon his prosp'rous Sword; approving Heav'n
Still Crown'd the Righteous Warrior with Success;
As if he said, Go forth, and be my Champion,
Thou most like me of all my Works below.

**PRINCE of TANAIS**
No lust of Rule, the common Vice of Kings,
No furious Zeal inspir'd by hot-brain'd Priests,
Ill hid beneath Religion's specious Name,
E'er drew his temp'rate. Courage to the Field:
But to redress an injur'd People's Wrongs,
To save the weak One from the strong Oppressor,
Is all his end of War; and when he draws
The Sword to punish, like relenting Heav'n,
He seems unwilling to deface his Kind.

**MIRVAN**
So rich his Soul in every virtuous Grace,
That, had not Nature made him great by Birth,
Yet all the Brave had sought him for their Friend:
The Christian Prince Axalla, nicely bred
In polish'd Arts of Europaean Courts,
For him forsakes his native Italy,
And lives a happy Exile in his Service.

**PRINCE of TANAIS**
Pleas'd with the gentle Manners of that Prince,
Our mighty Lord is lavish to his Friendship;
Tho' Omar, and the Tartar Lords repine,
And loudly tax their Monarch, as too partial.

**ZAMA**
E'er the mid Hour of Night, from Tent to Tent,

Unweary'd, thro' the num'rous Host he past,
Viewing with careful Eyes each sev'ral Quarter;
Whilst from his Looks, as from Divinity,
The Soldiers took presage; and cry'd, Lead on,
Great Alha, and our Emperor, Lead on,
To Victory, and Everlasting Fame.

**MIRVAN**
Hear you of Bajazet?

**PRINCE of TANAIS**
Late in the Evening
A Slave, of near Attendance on his Person,
'Scap'd to our Camp: from him we learn'd, the Tyrant
With Rage redoubled, for the Fight prepares;
Some accidental Passion fires his Breast,
(Love, as 'tis thought, for a fair Grecian Captive)
And adds new Horror to his native Fury;
For five returning Suns, scarce was he seen
By any the most favour'd of his Court;
But in lascivious Ease, among his Women,
Liv'd from the War retir'd; or else, alone
In sullen mood sate meditating Plagues,
And Ruin to the World, 'till yester Morn,
Like Fire that lab'ring upwards rends the Earth,
He burst with Fury from his Tent, Commanding
All should be ready for the Fight, this Day.

**ZAMA**
I know his Temper well, since, in his Court
Companion of the brave Axalla's Embassy,
I oft observ'd him, Proud, Impatient,
Of Ought Superiour, ev'n of Heav'n, that made him.
Fond of false Glory, of the Salvage Pow'r
Of ruling without Reason, of confounding
Just, and Unjust, by an Unbounded Will;
By whom Religion, Honour, all the Bands
That ought to hold the jarring World in Peace,
Were held the Tricks of State, Snares of wise Princes
To draw their easie Neighbours to Destruction.

**MIRVAN**
Thrice, by our Law and Prophet, has he sworn,
By the World's Lord, and Maker, lasting Peace
With our great Master, and his Royal Friend
The Grecian Emperor; as oft regardless
Of plighted Faith, with most Un-Kingly Baseness,
H' has ta'en th' Advantage of their absent Arms,

Without a War proclaim'd, or Cause pretended,
To waste with Sword and Fire their fruitful Fields:
Like some accursed Fiend, who 'scap'd from Hell,
Poisons the balmy Air thro' which he flies,
He blasts the bearded Corn, and loaded Branches,
The lab'ring Hind's best hopes, and marks his way with ruin.

**PRINCE of TANAIS**
But see! his Fate, the mighty Tamerlane
Comes like the Proxy of enquiring Heav'n,
To Judge, and to Redress.

[Flourish of Trumpets.

[Enter **TAMERLANE**, **GUARDS**, and other **ATTENDANTS**.

**TAMERLANE**
Yet, yet, a little and destructive Slaughter
Shall rage around, and marr this beauteous Prospect;
Pass but an hour, which stands betwixt the Lives
Of Thousands and Eternity: What Change
Shall hasty Death make in yon glitt'ring Plain?
Oh thou sell Monster, War! That in a moment
Lay'st waste the noblest part of the Creation,
The Boast, and Master-piece of the Great Maker,
That wears in vain th' Impression of his Image,
Unpriviledg'd from thee.
Health to our Friends, and to our Arms Success,
To the Prince, Zama and Mirvan
Such as the Cause for which we fight deserves.

**PRINCE of TANAIS**
Nor can we ask beyond what Heav'n bestows,
Preventing still our Wishes. See Great Sir!
The Universal Joy, your Soldiers wear,
Omen of prosp'rous Battle.
Impatient of the tedious Night in Arms
Watchful they stood expecting op'ning day;
And now are hardly by their Leaders held
From darting on the Foe; like a hot Courser,
That bounding Paws the mould'ring Soil, disdaining
The Rein that checks him, eager for the Race.

**TAMERLANE**
Yes, Prince, I mean to give a loose to War:
This Morn, Axalla, with my Parthian Horse
Arrives to joyn me, He, who like a Storm
Swept with his flying Squadrons all the Plain

Between Angoria's Walls, and yon tall Mountains
That seem to reach the Clouds; and now he comes
Loaden with Spoils, and Conquest, to my aid.

**ZAMA**
These Trumpets speak his Presence—

[Flourish of Trumpets.

[Enter **AXALLA** with **SOLDIERS. MONESES**, **STRATOCLES** and **SELIMA**, **PRISONERS**.

[**AXALLA** kneels to **TAMERLANE**.

**TAMERLANE**
Wellcome! thou worthy Partner of my Laurels,
Thou Brother of my Choice, a Band more Sacred
Than Nature's brittle Tye. By holy Friendship!
Glory, and Fame stood still for thy arrival,
My Soul seem'd wanting in its better half,
And languish'd for thy absence, like a Prophet,
That waits the Inspiration of his God.

**AXALLA**
My Emperor! my ever Royal Master!
To whom my Secret Soul more lowly bends,
Than Forms of outward Worship can express;
How poorly does your Soldier pay this Goodness,
Who wears his every hour of Life out for you?
Yet 'tis his All, and what he has he offers;
Nor now disdain, t' accept the Gift he brings,
This earnest of your Fortune. See my Lord
The noblest Prize, that ever grac'd my Arms;
Approach my Fair—

**TAMERLANE**
This is indeed to Conquer,
And well to be rewarded for thy Conquest;
The Bloom of opening Flow'rs, unsully'd Beauty,
Softness, and sweetest Innocence she wears,
And looks like Nature in the World's first Spring;
But say, Axalla—

**SELIMA**
Most Renown'd in War,

[Kneeling to **TAMERLANE**.

Look with Compassion on a Captive Maid,

[Kneeling to **TAMERLANE**.

Tho' born of Hostile Blood; nor let my Birth
Deriv'd from Bajazet, prevent that Mercy,
Which every Subject of your Fortune finds;
War is the Province of Ambitious Man,
Who tears the miserable World for Empire;
Whilst our weak Sex, incapable of wrong,
On either side claims Priviledge of Safety.

**TAMERLANE** [Raising her]
Rise, Royal Maid, the pride of haughty Pow'r,
Pays Homage, not receives it from the Fair:
Thy Angry Father fiercely calls me forth,
And urges me unwillingly to Arm;
Yet, tho' our frowning Battles menace Death
And mortal Conflict, think not that we hold
Thy Innocence and Virtue as our Foe.
Here, 'till the Fate of Asia is decided,
In safety stay. To Morrow is your own:
Nor grieve for who may Conquer, or who Lose;
Fortune on either side shall wait thy Wishes.

**SELIMA**
Where shall my Wonder and my Praise begin!
From the successful Labours of thy Arms?
Or from a Theme more soft, and full of Peace,
Thy Mercy, and thy Gentleness? Oh! Tamerlane!
What can I pay thee for this noble Usage
But greatful Praise? So Heav'n it self is paid.
Give Peace, ye Pow'rs above, Peace to Mankind
Not let my Father wage unequal War
Against the Force of such united Virtues.

**TAMERLANE**
Heav'n hear thy pious Wish!—But since our Prospect
Looks darkly on Futurity, 'till Fate
Determine for us, let thy Beauty's safety
Be my Axalla's Care; in whose glad Eyes
I read what Joy the pleasing Service gives him.
Is there amongst thy other Pris'ners ought
[To **AXALLA**.
Worthy our Knowledge?

**AXALLA**
This brave Man, my Lord,

[Pointing to **MONESES**.

With long resistance held the Combat doughtful:

[Pointing to **MONESES**.

His Party, prest with Numbers, soon grew faint,
And would have left their Charge an easie Prey;
Whilst he alone, undaunted at the odds,
Tho' hopeless to escape, fought well and firmly:
Nor yielded, 'till o'er match'd by many Hands,
He seem'd to shame our Conquest, whilst he own'd it.

**TAMERLANE**
Thou speak'st him as a Soldier should a Soldier,
Just to the worth he finds. I would not war
[To **MONESES**.
With ought that wears thy virtuous Stamp of Greatness:
Thy Habit speaks thee Christian—Nay, yet more,
My Soul seems pleas'd to take acquaintance with thee,
As if ally'd to thine: Perhaps 'tis Sympathy
Of honest Minds; like Strings wound up in Musick,
Where by one touch, both utter the same Harmony:
Why art thou then a Friend to Bajazet?
And why my Enemy?

**MONESES**
If human Wisdom
Could point out every Action of our Lives,
And say, Let it be thus, in spite of Fate,
Or partial Fortune, then I had not been
The Wretch I am.

**TAMERLANE**
The Brave meet every Accident
With equal Minds: Think nobler of thy Foes,
Than to account thy Chance in War an Evil.

**MONESES**
Far, far from that; I rather hold it grievous
That I was forc'd ev'n but to seem your Enemy;
Nor think the baseness of a vanquish'd Slave
Moves me to slatter for precarious Life,
Or ill-bought Freedom, when I swear by Heav'n!
Were I to chuse from all Mankind a Master,
It should be Tamerlane.

**TAMERLANE**

A noble Freedom
Dwells with the Brave, unknown to fawning Sycophants,
And Claims a Privilege of being believ'd.
I take thy Praise as earnest of thy Friendship.

**MONESES**
Still you prevent the Homage I should offer,
O Royal Sir! let my Misfortunes plead,
And wipe away the hostile Mark I wore.—
I was, when not long since my Fortune hail'd me,
Bless'd to my wish, I was the Prince Moneses;
Born and bred up to Greatness: Witness the Blood
Which thro' successive Hero's Veins ally'd
To our Greek Emperors, roll'd down to me,
Feeds the bright Flame of Glory in my Heart.

**TAMERLANE**
Ev'n that! that Princely Tye should bind thee to me,
If Virtue were not more than all Alliance.

**MONESES**
I have a Sister, (Oh severe Remembrance!)
Our Noble Houses, nay, her Sexe's Pride:
Nor think my Tongue too lavish, if I speak her
Fair as the Fame of Virtue, and yet chaste
As its cold Precepts, wise beyond her Sex
And blooming Youth, soft as forgiving Mercy,
Yet greatly brave, and jealous for her Honour:
Such as she was, to say I barely lov'd her,
Is poor to my Soul's meaning: From our Infancy
There grew a mutual Tenderness between us,
'Till not long since her Vows were kindly plighted
To a young Lord, the Equal of her Birth.
The happy Day was fix'd, and now approaching,
When faithless Bajazet (upon whose Honour,
In solemn Treaty giv'n, the Greeks depended)
With sudden War broke in upon the Country,
Secure of Peace, and for Defence unready.

**TAMERLANE**
Let Majesty no more be held Divine,
Since Kings, who are call'd Gods, profane themselves.

**MONESES**
Among the Wretches, whom that Deluge swept
Away to Slavery, my self and Sister
Then passing near the Frontiers to the Court,
(Which waited for her Naptials) were surpriz'd,

And made the Captives of the Tyrant's Power
Soon as we reach'd his Court, we found our Usage
Beyond what we expected, fair, and noble:
'Twas then the Storm of your victorious Arms
Look'd black, and seem'd to threaten, when he press'd me
(By oft repeated Instances) to draw
My Sword for him? But when he found my Soul
Disdain'd his Purpose, he more fiercely told me,
That my Arpasia, my lov'd Sister's Fate
Depended on my Courage shewn for him.
I had long learnt to hold my self at nothing,
But for her sake; to ward the Blow from her,
I bound my Service to the Man I hated.
Six Days are past, since by the Sultan's Order
I left the Pledge of my return behind,
And went to guard this Princess to his Camp:
The rest the brave Axalla's Fortune tells you.

**TAMERLANE**
Wisely the Tyrant strove, to prop his Cause
By leaguing with thy Virtue; but just Heav'n
Has torn thee from his Side, and left him naked
To the avenging Bolt that drives upon him:
Forget the Name of Captive, and I wish
I could as well restore that Fair One's Freedom,
Whose loss hangs heavy on thee: Yet e'er Night
Perhaps we may deserve thy Friendship nobler;
Th' approaching Storm may cast thy Shipwreck'd Wealth
Back to thy Arms: 'Till that be past, since War
(Tho' in the justest Cause) is ever doubtful,
I will not ask thy Sword to aid my Victory,
Lest it should hurt that Hostage of thy Valour
Our common Foe detains.

**MONESES**
Let Bajazet
Bend to his Yoak repining Slaves by sorce,
You, Sir, have found a nobler way to Empire,
Lord of the willing World.

**TAMERLANE**
Oh, my Axalla!
Thou hast a tender Soul, apt for Compassion,
And art thy self a Lover and a Friend:
Does not this Prince's Fortune move thy Temper?

**AXALLA**
Yes, Sir, I mourn the brave Moneses Fate;

The Merit of his Virtue hardly match'd
With disadvent'rous Chance: Yet, Prince, allow me,
Allow me from th' Experience of a Lover
To say, one Person, whom your Story mention'd,
(If he survive) is far beyond you wretched:
You nam'd the Bridegroom of your beauteous Sister.

**MONESES**
I did: Oh, most accurst!

**AXALLA**
Think what he feels,
Dash'd in the fierceness of his Expectation;
Then, when th' approaching Minute of Possession
Had wound Imagination to the heighth,
Think if he lives!—

**MONESES**
He lives, he does; 'tis true
He lives; but how? To be a Dog, and dead,
Were Paradise to such a State as his:
He holds down Life as Children do a Potion,
With strong Reluctance, and convulsive Strugglings,
Whilst his Misfortunes press him to disgorge it.

**TAMERLANE**
Spare the remembrance; 'tis a useless Grief,
And adds to the Misfortune by repeating it.
The revolution of a Day may bring
Such Turns, as Heav'n it self could scarce have promis'd,
Far, far beyond thy Wish: Let that Hope chear thee;
Haste my Axalla, to dispose, with safety,
Thy beauteous Charge, and on the Foe revenge
The Pain, which Absence gives; thy other care,
Honour and Arms, now summon thy Attendance;
Now, do thy Office well, my Soul, remember
Thy Cause; the Cause of Heav'n and injur'd Earth.
O thou Supream! if thy great Spirit warms
My glowing Breast, and fires my Soul to Arms,
Grant that my Sword, assisted by thy Pow'r,
This Day may Peace and Happiness restore,
That War and lawless Rage may vex thy World no more.

[Exeunt **TAMERLANE**, **MONESES**, **STRATOCLES**, **PRINCE of TANAIS**, **ZAMA**, **MIRVAN**, and **ATTENDANTS**.

[Manent **AXALLA**, and **SELIMA**, with **SOLDIERS**.

**AXALLA**

The Battle calls, and bids me hasse to leave thee
Oh! But let Destruction [.....]
Are there not Hours enough for Blood and Slaughter?
This moment shall be Love's, and I will waste it
In soft Complainings, for thy Sighs and Coldness,
For thy forgetful Coldness; even at Birza,
When in thy Father's Court my Eyes first own'd thee,
Fairer than Light, the Joy of their beholding,
Ev'n then thou wert not thus?

**SELIMA**
Art not thou chang'd?
Christian Axalla, Art thou still the same?
Those were the gentle Hours of Peace, and thou
The World's good Angel, that didst kindly join
Its mighty Masters in harmonious Friendship:
But since those Joys, that once were ours, are lost,
Forbear to mention 'em, and talk of War:
Talk of thy Conquest, and my Chains, Axalla.

**AXALLA**
Yet I will listen, fair unkind Upbraider,
Yet I will listen to thy charming Accents,
Altho' they make me curse my Fame and Fortune,
My Laurel-wreaths, and all the glorious Trophies,
For which the Valiant bleed—Oh! thou unjust one,
Dost thou then envy me this small return
My niggard Fate has made for all the Mournings,
For all the Pains, for all the sleepless Nights
That cruel Absence brings?

**SELIMA**
Away, Deceiver;
I will not hear thy soothing: Is it thus
That Christian Lovers prove the Faith they swear?
Are War and Slavery the soft Endearments
With which they Court the Beauties they admire?
'Twas well my Heart was cautious of believing
Thy Vows, and thy Protesting. Know my Conqueror,
Thy Sword has vanquish'd but the half of Selima,
Her Soul disdains thy Victory.

**AXALLA**
Hear, sweet Heav'n,
Hear the fair Tyrant, how she wrests Love's Laws,
As she had vow'd my Ruin! What is Conquest?
What Joy have I from that but to behold thee,
To kneel before thee, and with lifted Eyes

To view thee, as Devotion does a Saint,
With awful, trembling Pleasure: Then to swear
Thou art the Queen and Mistress of my Soul?
Has not ev'n Tamerlane (whose Word, next Heav'ns,
Makes Fate at second hand) bid thee disclaim
Thy Fears? And dost thou call thy self a Slave?
Only to try how far the sad Impression
Can sink into Axalla.

**SELIMA**
Oh Axalla!
Ought I to hear you?

**AXALLA**
Come back, ye Hours,
And tell my Selima what she has done:
Bring back the time, when to her Father's Court
I came Ambassador of Peace from Tamerlane;
When hid by conscious Darkness and Disguise,
I past the Dangers of the watchful Guards;
Bold as the Youth who nightly swam the Hellespont:
Then, then she was not sworn the Foe of Love;
When, as my Soul confest its Flame, and su'd
In moving sounds for Pity, she frown'd rarely,
But, blushing, heard me tell the gentle Tale:
Nay, ev'n confest, and told me softly sighing
She thought there was no guilt in Love like mine.

**SELIMA**
Young and unskilful in the World's false Arts,
I suffer'd Love to steal upon my Softness,
And warm me with a lambent guiltless Flame:
Yes, I have heard thee swear a thousand times,
And call the conscious Pow'rs of Heav'n to witness
The tend'rest, truest, everlasting Passion:
But, Oh! 'tis past; and I will charge Remembrance
To banish the sond Image from my Soul:
Since thou art sworn the Foe of Royal Bajazet,
I have resolv'd to hate thee.

**AXALLA**
Is it possible!
Hate is not in thy Nature; thy whole Frame
Is Harmony, without one jarring Atom.
Why do'st thou sorce thy Eyes to wear this Coldness
It damps the Springs of Life. Oh! bid me die,
Much rather bid me die, if it be true,
That thou hast sworn to hate me.—

**SELIMA**
Let Life and Death
Wait the Decision of the bloody Field;
Nor can thy Fate (my Conqueror) depend
Upon a Woman's Hate. Yet since you urge
A Power, which once perhaps I had, there is
But one Request, that I can make with Honour.

**AXALLA**
Oh! name it! say!—

**SELIMA**
Forego your right of War,
And render me this instant to my Father.

**AXALLA**
Impossible!—The tumult of the Battle,
That hastes to joyn, cuts off all means of Commerce
Betwixt the Armies.

**SELIMA**
Swear then to perform it,
Which way soe'er the chance of War determines,
On my first instance.

**AXALLA**
By the sacred Majesty
Of Heav'n, to whom we kneel, I will obey thee;
Yes, I will give thee this severest Proof
Of my Soul's vow'd Devotion, I will part with thee
(Thou Cruel, to command it!) I will part with thee,
As Wretches, that are doubtful of Hereafter,
Part with their Lives, unwilling, loth and fearful,
And trembling at Futurity. But is there nothing,
No small return that Honour can afford
For all this waste of Love?

**SELIMA**
The Gifts of Captives
Wear somewhat of Constraint; and generous Minds
Disdain to give, where freedom of the Choice
Does but seem wanting.

**AXALLA**
What! not one kind Look?
Then thou art chang'd indeed.

[Trumpets.

Hark! I am summon'd
And thou wilt send me forth like one unbless'd;
Whom Fortune has forsaken, and ill Fate
Mark'd for Destruction. Thy surprising Coldness
Hangs on my Soul, and weighs my Courage down;
And the first feeble Blow I meet shall raze me
From all Remembrance: Nor is Life or Fame
Worthy my Care, since I am lost to thee.

[Going.

**SELIMA**
Ha! Goest thou to the Fight!—

**AXALLA**
I do.—Farewel!—

**SELIMA**
What! and no more! A Sigh heaves in my Breast,
And stops the struggling Accents on my Tongue,
Else, sure, I should have added something more,
And made our Parting softer.

**AXALLA**
Give it way,
The niggard Honour, that affords not Love,
Forbids not Pity—

**SELIMA**
Fate perphaps has set
This Day, the Period of thy Life, and Conquests,
And I shall see thee born at Evening back,
A breathless Coarse;—Oh! Can I think on that
And hide my Sorrows?—No—they will have way,
And all the Vital Air, that Life draws in,
Is render'd back in Sighs.

**AXALLA**
The murm'ring Gale revives the drooping Flame,
That at thy Coldness languish'd in my Breast;
So breath the gentle Zephyrs on the Spring,
And waken every Plant, and od'rous Flower,
Which Winter Frosts had blasted, to new Life.

**SELIMA**
To see thee for this moment, and no more—

Oh! help me to resolve against this Tenderness,
That charms my fierce Resentments, and presents thee
Not as thou art, mine, and my Father's Foe,
But as thou wert, when first thy moving Accents
Won me to hear; when, as I listn'd to thee,
The happy Hours past by us unperceiv'd,
So was my Soul fix'd to the soft Enchantment.

**AXALLA**
Let me be still the same, I am, I must be.
If it were possible my Heart could stray,
One Look from thee would call it back again,
And fix the Wanderer for ever thine.

**SELIMA**
Where is my boasted Resolution now?

[Sinking into his Arms.

Oh! Yes! Thou art the same; my Heart joins with thee,

[Sinking into his Arms.

And to betray me will believe thee still:
It dances to the Sounds that mov'd it first,
And owns at once the weakness of my Soul:
So when some skilful Artist strikes the Strings,
The magick Numbers rouze our sleeping Passions,
And force us to confess our Grief, and Pleasure.
Alas! Axalla, say—dost thou not pity
My artless Innocence, and easie Fondness?
Oh! turn thee from me, or I die with blushing.

**AXALLA**
No—let me rather gaze, for ever gaze,
And bless the new-born Glories that adorn thee;
From every Blush, that kindles in thy Cheeks,
Ten thousand little Loves, and Graces spring,
To revel in the Roses—'two' not be,

[Trumpets.

This envious Trumpet calls, and tears me from thee—

**SELIMA**
My Fears increase, and doubly press me now,
I charge thee, if thy Sword comes cross my Father,
Stop for a moment, and remember me.

**AXALLA**

Oh! doubt not, but his Life shall be my care,
Ev'n dearer than my own—

**SELIMA**

Guard that for me too.

**AXALLA**

Oh! Selima! thou hast restor'd my quiet,
The noble ardour of the War, with Love
Returning, brightly burns within my Breast,
And bids me be secure of all hereafter.
So chears some pious Saint a dying Sinner,
(Who trembled at the thought of Pains to come)
With Heav'ns Forgiveness, and the hopes of Mercy:
At length the tumult of his Soul appeas'd,
And every Doubt, and anxious Scruple eas'd,
Boldly he proves the dark, uncertain Road,
The Peace, his holy Comforter bestow'd,
Guides, and protects him, like a guardian God.

[Exit **AXALLA**.

**SELIMA**

In vain all Arts a Love-sick Virgin tries,
Affects to frown, and seems severely wise,
In hopes to cheat the weary Lover's Eyes.
If the dear Youth her Pity strives to move,
And pleads, with tenderness, the cause of Love;
Nature asserts her Empire in her Heart,
And kindly takes the faithful Lover's part.
By Love, her self, and Nature thus betray'd,
No more she trusts in Pride's fantastick Aid,
But bids her Eyes confess the yielding Maid.

[Exit **SELIMA**, **GUARDS** following.

ACT II

SCENE I

SCENE Tamerlane's Camp

Enter **MONESES**.

**MONESES**

The dreadful Business of the War is over,
And slaughter, that, from yester Morn 'till Even,
With Giant Steps, past striding o'er the Field,
Besmear'd, and horrid with the Blood of Nations,
Now weary sits among the mangled Heaps,
And slumbers o'er her Prey; while from this Camp
The chearful Sounds of Victory, and Tamerlane,
Beat the high Arch of Heav'n; deciding Fate,
That Crowns him with the Spoils of such a Day,
Has giv'n it as an Earnest of the World
That shortly shall be his.

[Enter **STRATOCLES**.

My Stratocles!
Most happily return'd; might I believe
Thou bring'st me any Joy?

**STRATOCLES**

With my best Diligence,
This Night, I have enquir'd of what concerns you.
Scarce was the Sun, who shone upon the Horror
Of the past day, sunk to the Western Ocean,
When by permission from the Prince Axalla,
I mixt among the Tumult of the Warriors,
Returning from the Battle: Here a Troop
Of hardy Parthians red with honest Wounds,
Confest the Conquest, they had well deserv'd:
There a dejected Crew of wretched Captives
Sore with unprofitable Hurts, and groaning
Under new Bondage, follow'd sadly after
The haughty Victor's heels; but that, which fully
Crown'd the Success of Tamerlane, was Bajazet,
Fall'n like the proud Archangel from the height,
Where once (even next to Majesty Divine)
Enthron'd he sat, down to the vile Descent
And lowness of a Slave; but oh! to speak
The Rage, the Fierceness, and the Indignation!—
It bars all Words, and cuts Description short.

**MONESES**

Then he is fall'n! that Comet, which, on high,
Portended Ruin; he has spent his Blaze,
And shall distract the World with Fears no more:
Sure it must bode me well, for oft my Soul
Has started into Tumult at his Name,
As if my Guardian Angel took th' Alarm,

At the approach of somewhat mortal to me:
But say, my Friend, what hear'st thou of Arpasia?
For there my Thoughts, my every Care is center'd.

**STRATOCLES**
Tho' on that purpose still I bent my Search,
Yet nothing certain could I gain, but this,
That in the Pillage of the Sultan's Tent,
Some Women were made Pris'ners, who this Morning
Were to be offer'd to the Emperor's View;
Their Names, and Qualities, tho' oft enquiring,
I could not learn.

**MONESES**
Then must my Soul still labour
Beneath Uncertainty, and anxious Doubt,
The Mind's worst State. The Tyrant's Ruin gives me
But a Half-ease.

**STRATOCLES**
'Twas said, not far from hence
The Captives were to wait the Emperor's Passage.

**MONESES**
Haste me to find the Place. Oh! my Arpasia!
Shall we not meet? Why hangs my Heart thus heavy
Like Death within my Bosom? Oh! 'tis well,
The Joy of Meeting pays the Pangs of Absence,
Else who could bear it?
When thy lov'd Sight shall bless my Eyes again,
Then I will own, I ought not to complain,
Since that sweet Hour is worth whole Years of Pain.

[Exeunt **MONESES**, and **STRATOCLES**.


SCENE II. The Inside of a Magnificent Tent

[Symphony of Warlike Musick.

[Enter **TAMERLANE**, **AXALLA**, **PRINCE of TANAIS**, **ZAMA**, **MIRVAN**, **SOLDIERS** and other **ATTENDANTS**.

**AXALLA**
From this Auspicious Day the Parthian Name
Shall date its Birth of Empire, and extend
Ev'n from the dawning East to utmost Thulé
The Limits of its Sway.

**PRINCE of TANAIS**
Nations unknown,
Where yet the Roman Eagles never flew,
Shall pay their Homage to Victorious Tamerlane,
Bend to his Valour, and superior Virtue,
And own, that Conquest is not giv'n by Chance,
But, bound by fatal and resistless Merit,
Waits on his Arms.

**TAMERLANE**
It is too much, you dress me
Like an Usurper in the borrow'd Attributes
Of injur'd Heav'n: Can we call Conquest ours?
Shall Man this Pigmy with a Giant's Pride
Vaunt of himself, and say, Thus have I done this?
Oh! vain Pretence to Greatness! Like the Moon,
We borrow all the Brightness, which we boast,
Dark in our selves, and useless. If that Hand
That rules the Fate of Battles strike for us,
Crown us with Fame, and gild our Clay with Honour;
'Twere most ungrateful to disown the Benefit,
And arrogate a Praise which is not ours.

**AXALLA**
With such unshaken Temper of the Soul
To bear the swelling Tide of prosp'rous Fortune,
Is to deserve that Fortune: In Adversity
The Mind grows tough by buffeting the Tempest;
Which, in Success dissolving, sinks to ease,
And loses all her Firmness.

**TAMERLANE**
Oh! Axalla!
Could I forget I am a Man, as thou art,
Would not the Winter's Cold, or Summer's Heat,
Sickness, or Thirst, and Hunger, all the Train
Of Nature's clamorous Appetites asserting
An Equal Right in Kings, and common men,
Reprove me daily?—No—If I boast of ought,
Be it, to have been Heaven's happy Instrument,
The means of Good to all my Fellow-Creatures;
This is a King's best Praise.

[Enter **OMAR**.

**OMAR**
Honour and Fame

[Bowing to **TAMERLANE**.

For ever wait the Emperor; may our Prophet
Give him ten thousand thousand Days of Life,
And every Day like this. The Captive Sultan
Fierce in his Bonds, and at his Fate repining,
Attends your sacred Will.

**TAMERLANE**
Let him approach.

[Enter **BAJAZET** and other **TURKISH PRISONERS** in Chains, with a Guard of **SOLDIERS**.

When I survey the Ruins of this Field,
The wild Destruction, which thy fierce Ambition
Has dealt among Mankind, (so many Widdows,
And helpless Orphans has thy Battle made,
That half our Eastern World this day are Mourners)
Well may I in behalf of Heav'n and Earth
Demand from thee Atonement for this wrong.

**BAJAZET**
Make thy Demand to those that own thy Pow'r,
Know I am still beyond it; and tho' Fortune
(Curse on that Changeling Deity of Fools!)
Has stript me of the Train, and Pomp of Greatness,
That out-side of a King, yet still my Soul,
Fixt high, and of it self alone dependant,
Is ever Free, and Royal, and ev'n now,
As at the head of Battle does desie thee:
I know what Pow'r the Chance of War has giv'n,
And dare thee to the use on't. This vile Speeching,
This After-game of Words is what most irks me;
Spare that, and for the rest 'tis equal all—
Be it as it may.

**TAMERLANE**
Well was it for the World,
When on their Borders Neighbouring Princes met,
Frequent in Friendly Parle, by cool Debates,
Preventing wasteful War; such should our Meeting
Have been, had'st thou but held in just regard
The Sanctity of Leagues so often sworn to,
Can'st thou believe thy Prophet, or what's more,
That Pow'r Supream, which made thee, and thy Prophet,
Will, with Impunity, let pass that Breach
Of sacred Faith giv'n to the Royal Greek?

**BAJAZET**
Thou Pedant Talker! ha! art thou a King
Possest of sacred Pow'r, Heav'ns darling Attribute,
And dost thou prate of Leagues, and Oaths, and Prophets?
I hate the Greek (Perdition on his Name!)
As I do thee, and would have met you both,
As Death does human Nature, for Destruction.

**TAMERLANE**
Causeless to hate is not of human kind;
The salvage Brute, that haunts in Woods remote,
And Desart-wilds, tears not the fearful Traveller,
If Hunger, or some Injury provoke not.

**BAJAZET**
Can a King want a Cause when Empire bids
Go on? what is he born for but Ambition?
It is his Hunger, 'tis his Call of Nature,
The Noble Appetite which will be satisfy'd,
And like the Food of Gods, makes him Immortal.

**TAMERLANE**
Henceforth I will not wonder we were Foes,
Since Souls that differ so, by Nature hate,
And strong Antipathy forbids their Union.

**BAJAZET**
The noble Fire that warms me does indeed
Transcend thy Coldness, I am pleas'd we differ,
Nor think alike.

**TAMERLANE**
No—for I think like Man
Thou like a Monster; from whose baleful Presence
Nature starts back; and tho' she six'd her Stamp
On thy rough Mass, and mark'd thee for a Man,
Now conscions of her Error, she disclaims thee,
As form'd for her Destruction.—
'Tis true, I am a King, as thou hast been:
Honour, and Glory too have been my aim;
But tho' I dare face Death, and all the Dangers,
Which furious War wears in its bloody Front,
Yet would I chuse to fix my Fame by Peace,
By Justice, and by Mercy; and to raise
My Trophies on the Blessings of Mankind;
Nor would I buy the Empire of the World
With Ruin of the People whom I sway,

Or Forfeit of my Honour.

**BAJAZET**
Prophet, I thank thee.—
Damnation!—Could'st thou rob me of my Glory,
To dress up this tame King, this preaching Dervise?
Unfit for War, thou should'st have liv'd secure
In lazy Peace, and with debating Senates
Shar'd a precarious Scepter, sate tamely still,
And let bold Factions canton out thy Pow'r,
And wrangle for the Spoils they robb'd thee of;
Whilst I (curse on the Power that stops my Ardour!)
Would, like a Tempest, rush amidst the Nations,
Be greatly terrible, and deal, like Alha,
My angry Thunder on the frighted World.

**TAMERLANE**
The World!—'twould be too little for thy Pride:
Thou would'st scale Heav'n—

**BAJAZET**
I would:—Away: my Soul
Disdains thy Conference.

**TAMERLANE**
Thou vain, rash Thing,
That, with gigantick Insolence, hast dar'd
To lift thy wretched self above the Stars,
And mate with Pow'r Almighty: Thou art fallen!—

**BAJAZET**
'Tis false! I am not fall'n from ought I have been;
At least my Soul resolves to keep her State,
And scorns to take Acquaintance with ill Fortune.

**TAMERLANE**
Almost beneath my Pity art thou fall'n;
Since, while th' avenging Hand of Heav'n is on thee,
And presses to the Dust thy swelling Soul,
Fool-hardy, with the stronger thou contendest;
To what vast heights had thy tumultuous Temper
Been hurry'd, if Success had crown'd thy Wishes;
Say, What had I to expect, if thou had'st conquer'd?

**BAJAZET**
Oh, Glorious Thought! By Heav'n! I will enjoy it,
Tho' but in Fancy; Imagination shall
Make room to entertain the vast Idea.

Oh! had I been the Master but of Yesterday,
The World, the World had felt me; and for thee,
I had us'd thee, as thou art to me,—a Dog,
The Object of my Scorn, and mortal Hatred:
I would have taught thy Neck to know my weight,
And mounted from that Footstool to my Saddle:
Then, when thy daily servile Task was done,
I would have cag'd thee, for the Scorn of Slaves,
'Till thou had'st begg'd to die; and ev'n that Mercy
I had deny'd Thee: Now thou know'st my Mind,
And question me no farther.

**TAMERLANE**
Well dost thou teach me
What Justice should exact from thee: Mankind
With one Consent cry out for Vengeance on thee;
Loudly they call, to cut off this League-breaker,
This wild Destroyer, from the Face of Earth.

**BAJAZET**
Do it, and rid thy shaking Soul at once
Of its worst Fear.

**TAMERLANE**
Why slept the Thunder,
That should have arm'd thy Idol Deity,
And given thee Pow'r, e're yester Sun was set,
To shake the Soul of Tamerlane: Had'st thou an Arm
To make thee fear'd, thou should'st have prov'd it on me,
Amidst the Sweat and Blood of yonder Field,
When, thro' the Tumult of the War, I sought thee,
Fenc'd in with Nations.

**BAJAZET**
Curse upon the Stars,
That fated us to different Scenes of Slaughter!
Oh! could my Sword have met thee!—

**TAMERLANE**
Thou had'st then,
As now, been in my Pow'r, and held thy Life
Dependant on my Gift.—Yes Bajazet,
I bid thee, Live.—So much my Soul disdains,
That thou should'st think, I can fear ought but Heav'n:
Nay more; could'st thou forget thy brutal fierceness,
And form thy self to Manhood, I would bid thee,
Live, and be still a King, that thou may'st learn
What Man should be to Man, in War remembring

The Common Tye, and Brotherhood of Kind.
This Royal Tent, with such of thy Domesticks,
As can be found, shall wait upon thy Service;
Nor will I use my Fortune, to demand
Hard Terms of Peace, but such as thou may'st offer
With Honour, I with Honour may receive,

[TAMERLANE signs to an OFFICER, who unbinds BAJAZET.

**BAJAZET**
Ha! say'st thou—no!—our Prophet's Vengeance blast me,
If thou shalt buy my Friendship with thy Empire.
Damnation on thee! thou smooth, fawning Talker!
Give me again my Chains, that I may curse thee,
And gratifie my Rage: Or, if thou wilt,
Be a vain Fool, and play with thy Perdition,
Remember I'm thy Foe, and hate thee deadly.
Thy Folly on thy Head!

**TAMERLANE**
Be still my Foe;
Great Minds (like Heav'n) are pleas'd in doing good,
Tho' the ungrateful Subjects of their Favours
Are barren in return: Thy stubborn Pride
That spurns the gentle Office of Humanity,
Shall, in my Honour own, and thy Despite,
I have done, as I ought. Virtue still does
With Scorn, the Mercenary World regard,
Where abject Souls do good, and hope reward:
Above the worthless Trophies Men can raise,
She seeks not Honours, Wealth, nor airy Praise,
But with her self, Her self, the Goddess pays.

[Exeunt TAMERLANE, AXALLA, PRINCE of TANAIS, MIRVAN, ZAMA, and ATTENDANTS.

[Manent BAJAZET, OMAR, GUARDS.

**BAJAZET**
Come, lead me to my Dungeon; plunge me down,
Deep from the hated Sight of Man, and Day,
Where, under Covert of the friendly Darkness,
My Soul may brood, at leisure, o'er its Anguish.

**OMAR**
Our Royal Master wou'd, with noble Usage,
Make your Misfortunes light, he bids you hope.—

**BAJAZET**

I tell thee, Slave, I have shook hands with Hope,
And all my Thoughts are Rage, Despair, and Horror,

[Enter **HALY**, **ARPASIA**, and **WOMEN ATTENDANTS**.

Ha! wherefore am I thus?—Perdition seize me!
But my cold Blood runs shiv'ring to my Heart,
As at some Fantom, that in dead of Night,
With dreadful Action stalks around our Beds.
The Rage, and fiercer Passions of my Breast
Are lost in new Confusion.—Arpasia!—Haly!

**HALY**
Oh, Emperor! for whose hard Fate our Prophet,
And all the Heroes of thy sacred Race
Are sad in Paradise, thy faithful Haly,
The Slave of all thy Pleasures, in this Ruin,
This Universal Shipwreck of thy Fortunes,
Has gather'd up this Treasure for thy Arms:
Nor ev'n the Victor, haughty Tamerlane,
(By whose Command, once more, thy Slave beholds thee)
Denies this Blessing to thee, but with Honour
Renders thee back thy Queen, thy beauteous Bride.

**BAJAZET**
Oh! had her Eyes, with pity, seen my Sorrows,
Had she the softness of a tender Bride,
Heav'n cou'd not have bestow'd a greater Blessing,
And Love had made amends for loss of Empire.
But see, what Fury dwells upon her Charms!
What Lightning flashes from her angry Eyes!
With a malignant Joy she views my Ruin:
Ev'n Beauteous in her Hatred, still she charms me,
And awes my fierce tumultuous Soul to Love.

**ARPASIA**
And dar'st thou hope, thou Tyrant! Ravisher!
That Heav'n has any Joy in store for thee?
Look back upon the Sum of thy past Life,
Tyranny, Oppression, and Injustice,
[.....], Murders, swell the black [.....],
Where lost Arpasia's [.....]
Thy last[.....]
At length the [.....]
My weary Soul shall be a little longer
The pain of Life, to call for Justice on [.....]
That once compleat, sink to the peaceful Grave,
And lose the memory of my Wrongs and Thee

**BAJAZET**
Thou rail'st! I thank thee for it—Be perverse,
And muster all the Women in thy Soul;
Goad me with Curses, be a very Wife,
That I may fling off this tame Love, and hate thee.

[Enter **MONESES**.

[**BAJAZET** starting.

Ha!—Keep thy temper Heart; nor take alarm
At a Slave's Presence.

**MONESES**
It is Arpasia!—Leave me, thou cold Fear.
Sweet as the rosie Morn she breaks upon me,
And Sorrow, like the Night's unwholsome Shade,
Gives way before the Golden Dawn she brings.

**BAJAZET** [Advancing towards him]
Ha, Christian! Is it well that we meet thus?
Is this thy Faith?

**MONESES**
Why does thy frowning Brow
Put on this form of Fury? Is it strange
We should meet here Companions in Misfortune,
The Captives of one common Chance of War?
Nor should'st thou wonder, that my Sword has fail'd
Before the Fortune of Victorious Tamerlane,
When thou with Nations like the sanded Shore,
With half the warring World upon thy side,
Could'st not stand up against his dreadful Battle,
That crush'd thee with its shock. Thy Men can witness,
Those Cowards, that forsook me in the Combat
My Sword was not unactive.

**BAJAZET**
No,—'tis false.
Where is my Daughter, thou vile Greek? thou hast
Betray'd her to the Tartar; or even worse,
Pale with thy Fears, didst lose her like a Coward;
And like a Coward now, would'st cast the blame
On Fortune, and ill Stars.

**MONESES**
Ha! said'st thou like a Coward?

What Sanctity, what Majesty Divine
Hast thou put on, to guard thee from my Rage?
That thus thou dar'st to wrong me.

**BAJAZET**
Silence, thou Slave,
And know me for thy Lord—

**MONESES**
I tell thee, Tyrant,
When in the Pride of Pow'r thou sat'st on high,
When like an Idol thou wert vainly worshipp'd,
By prostrate Wretches, born with slavish Souls:
Ev'n when thou wert a King, thou wert not more,
Nor greater than Moneses; born of a Race
Royal, and Great as thine: What art thou now then?
The Fate of War has set thee with the Lowest;
And Captives (like the Subjects of the Grave)
Losing distinction, serve one common Lord.

**BAJAZET**
Brav'd by this Dog! now give a loose to Rage,
And curse thy self, curse thy false, cheating Prophet.
Ha! Yet there's some Revenge. Hear me, thou Christian,
Thou left'st that Sister with me:—Thou Impostor!
Thou Boaster of thy Honesty! Thou Lyar!
But take her to thee back.
Now to explore my Prison.—If it holds
Another Plague like this, the restless Damn'd
(If Mufty's lie not) wander thus in Hell?
From scorching Flames to chilling Frosts they run,
Then from their Frosts to Fires return again,
And only prove variety of Pain.

[Exeunt **BAJAZET** and **HALY**.

**ARPASIA**
Stay, Bajazet, I charge thee by my Wrongs!
Stay, and unfold a Tale of so much Horror,
As only sits thy telling.—Oh, Moneses!

**MONESES**
Why dost thou weep? why this tempestuous Passion,
That stops thy falt'ring Tongue short on my Name?
Oh, speak! unveil this Mystery of Sorrow,
And draw the dismal Scene, at once, to sight,

**ARPASIA**

Thou art undone, lost, ruin'd, and undone.

**MONESES**
I will not think 'tis so, while I have thee,
While thus 'tis giv'n to fold thee in my Arms;
For while I sigh upon thy panting Bosom,
The sad remembrance of past Woes is lost.

**ARPASIA**
Forbear to sooth thy Soul with flatt'ring Thoughts
Of Evils overpast, and Joys to come:
Our Woes are like the genuine Shade beneath,
Where Fate cuts off the very hopes of Day,
And everlasting Night and Horror reign.

**MONESES**
By all the Tenderness, and chaste Endearments
Of our past Love, I charge thee, my Arpasia,
To case my Soul of Doubts; give me to know
At once the utmost Malice of my Fate.

**ARPASIA**
Take then thy wretched Share in all I suffer,
Still Partner of my Heart. Scarce had'st thou left
The Sultan's Camp, when the Imperious Tyrant,
Softning the pride and fierceness of his Temper,
With gentle Speech made offer of his Love.
Amaz'd, as at the shock of sudden Death,
I started into Tears, and often urg'd
(Tho' still in vain) the difference of our Faiths:
At last, as flying to the utmost Refuge,
With lifted Hands, and streaming Eyes, I own'd
The Fraud; which when we first were made his Pris'ners,
Conscious of my unhappy Form, and fearing
For thy dear Life, I forc'd thee to put on
Thy borrow'd Name of Brother, mine of Sister;
Hiding beneath that Veil the nearer Tie,
Our mutual Vows had made before the Priest;
Kindling to Rage at hearing of my Story,
Then be it so. Think'st thou thy Vows
Giv'n to a Slave shall bar me from thy Beauties?
Then bad the Priest pronounce the Marriage Rites,
Which he perform'd, whilst shrieking with Despair,
I call'd in vain the Pow'rs of Heav'n to aid me.

**MONESES**
Villain! Imperial Villain!—Oh, the Coward!
Aw'd by his Guilt, tho' back'd by Force and Power,

He durst not to my Face avow his Purpose;
But in my absence like a lurking [.....]
Stole on my Treasure, and at once undid me.

**ARPASIA**
Had they not kept me from the means of Death,
Forgetting all the Rules of Christian Suffering,
I had done a desp'rate Murder on my Soul,
E'er the rude Slaves, that waited on his Will,
Had forc'd me to his—

**MONESES**
Stop thee there, Arpasia,
And bar my Fancy from the guilty Scene;
Let not Thought enter, lest the busie Mind
Should muster such a train of monstrous Images,
As wou'd distract me. Oh! I cannot bear it.
Thou lovely Hoard of Sweets, where all my Joy,
Were treasur'd up, to have thee rifled thus!
Thus torn untasted from my eager Wishes!
But I will have thee from him. Tamerlane
(The Sovereign Judge of Equity on Earth)
Shall do me Justice on this mighty Robber,
And render back thy Beauties to Moneses.

**ARPASIA**
And who shall render back my Peace, my Honour,
The spotless Whiteness of my Virgin Soul?
Ah! no, Moneses—think not I will ever
Bring a polluted Love to thy chaste Arms:
I am the Tyrant's Wife. Oh, fatal Title!
And, in the sight of all the Saints, have sworn,
By Honour, Womanhood, and blushing Shame,
To know no second Bride-bed, but my Grave.

**MONESES**
I swear it must not be, since still my Eye
Finds thee as heav'nly white, as Angel pure,
As in the earliest hours of Life, thou wert,
Nor art thou his, but mine; thy first Vow's mine,
Thy Soul is mine,—

**ARPASIA**
Oh! think not, that the Pow'r
Of most persuasive Eloquence can make me
Forget, I've been another's, been his Wife;
Now by my Blushes! by the strong Confusion,
And Anguish of my Heart! spare me Moneses,

Nor urge my trembling Virtue to the Precipice.
Shortly, (oh! very shortly) if my Sorrows
Divine aright, and Heav'n be gracious to me,
Death shall dissolve the fatal Obligation,
And give me up to Peace, to that blest Place
Where the Good rest from Care and anxious Life.

**MONESES**
Oh! teach me, thou fair Saint, like thee to suffer,
Teach me, with hardy Piety, to combat
The present Ills, instruct my Eyes to pass
The narrow bounds of Life, this Land of Sorrow,
And with bold Hopes, to view the Realms beyond,
Those distant Beauties of the future State.
Tell me Arpasia,—say, what Joys are those,
That wait to crown the Wretch who suffers here
Oh! tell me, and sustain my sailing Faith.

**ARPASIA**
Imagine somewhat exquisitly fine,
Which Fancy cannot paint, which the pleas'd Mind
Can barely know, unable to describe it;
Imagine, 'tis a Tract of endless Joys,
Without Satiety, or Interruption;
Imagine, 'tis to meet, and part no more.

**MONESES**
Grant, gentle Heaven, that such may be our Lot!
Let us be blest together,—Oh! my Soul!
Build on that hope, and let it arm thy Courage,
To struggle with the Storm, that parts us now.

**ARPASIA**
Yes! my Moneses, now the Surges rise,
The swelling Sea breaks in between our Barks,
And drives us to our Fate on different Rocks,
Farewel!—my Soul lives with thee.—

**MONESES**
Death is parting,
'Tis the last sad Adieu 'twixt Soul and Body,
But this is somewhat worse—my Joy, my Comfort,
All that was left in Life fleets after thee.
My aking Sight hangs on thy parting Beauties,
Thy lovely Eyes all drown'd in Floods of Sorrow!
So sinks the setting Sun beneath the Waves,
And leaves the Traveller in pathless Woods,
Benighted and forlorn,—Thus with sad Eyes

Westward he turns, to mark the Light's decay,
Till having lost the last faint Glimpse of Day,
Chearless, in darkness, he pursues his way.

[Exeunt **MONESES** and **ARPASIA** severally.

ACT III

SCENE I

SCENE, the Inside of the Royal Tent

Enter **AXALLA**, **SELIMA**, and **WOMEN ATTENDANTS**.

**AXALLA**
CAN there be ought in Love, beyond this Proof,
This wond'rous Proof, I give thee of my Faith?
To tear thee from my bleeding Bosom thus?
To rend the Strings of Life, to set thee free,
And yield thee to a cruel Father's Power,
Foe to my Hopes? What can'st thou pay me back,
What but thy self (thou Angel) for this Fondness?

**SELIMA**
Thou dost upbraid me, Beggar as I am,
And urge me with my Poverty of Love.
Perhaps thou think'st, 'tis nothing for a Maid
To struggle thro' the Niceness of her Sex,
The Blushes, and the Fears, and own she loves:
Thou think'st, 'tis nothing for my artless Heart
To own my Weakness, and confess thy Triumph.

**AXALLA**
Oh! yes, I own it; my charm'd Ears ne'er knew
A Sound of so much Rapture, so much Joy.
Not Voices, Instruments, not warbling Birds,
Not Winds, not murm'ring Waters join'd in Consort,
Not tuneful Nature, not th' according Spheres
Utter such Harmony, as when my Selima
With down cast Looks, and Blushes said,—I love—

**SELIMA**
And yet thou say'st, I am a Niggard to thee:
I swear the Ballance shall be held between us,
And Love be Judge, if after all the Tenderness,
Tears, and Confusion of my Virgin Soul,

Thou should'st complain of ought, Unjust Axalla!

**AXALLA**
Why was I ever blest?—Why is Remembrance
Rich with a thousand pleasing Images
Of past Enjoyments, since 'tis but to plague me?
When thou art mine no more, what will it ease me
To think of all the Golden Minutes past,
To think, that thou wert kind, and I was happy:
But like an Angel fall'n from Bliss, to curse
My present State, and mourn the Heav'n I've lost.

**SELIMA**
Hope better for us both; nor let thy Fears,
Like an unlucky Omen, cross my way.
My Father rough, and stormy in his Nature,
To me was always gentle, and, with Fondness
Paternal, ever met me with a Blessing.
Oft when Offence had stir'd him to such Fury,
That not grave Counsellors for Wisdom sam'd,
Nor hardy Captains that had sought his Battles,
Presum'd to speak, but struck with awful Dread,
Were hush'd as Death; yet has he smil'd on me,
Kill me, and bad me utter all my purpose;
Till, with my idle Prattle, I had sooth'd him,
And won him from his Anger.

**AXALLA**
Oh! I know,
Thou hast a Tongue to charm the wildest Tempers.
Herds would forget to graze, and Savage Beasts
Stand still, and lose their Fierceness, but to hear thee,
As if they had Reflection, and by Reason
Forsook a less Enjoyment for a greater.
But oh! when I revolve each Circumstance,
My Christian Faith, my Service closely bound
To Tamerlane my Master, and my Friend:
Tell me (my Charmer) if my Fears are vain?
Think what remains for me, if the fierce Sultan
Should doom thy Beauties to another's Bed?

**SELIMA**
'Tis a sad Thought, but to appease thy Doubts,
Here, in the awful Sight of Heav'n, I vow,
No Pow'r shall e'er divide me from thy Love,
Ev'n Duty shall not force me to be false.
My cruel Stars may tear thee from my Arms,
But never from my Heart; and when the Maids

Shall yearly come with Garlands of fresh Flow'rs,
To mourn with pious Office o'er my Grave,
They shall sit sadly down, and weeping tell,
How well I lov'd, how much I suffer'd for thee,
And while they grieve my Fate, shall praise my Constancy.

**AXALLA**
But see! the Sultan comes!—my beating Heart
Bounds with exulting Motion; Hope and Fear
Fight with alternate Conquest in my Breast.
Oh! Can I give her from me? Yield her up?
Now mourn, thou God of Love, since Honour triumphs,
And crowns his cruel Altars with thy Spoils.

[Enter **BAJAZET**.

**BAJAZET**
To have a nauseous Courtesie forc'd on me
Spight of my Will, by an insulting Foe,—
Ha! they wou'd break the Fierceness of my Temper,
And make me supple for their slavish purpose:
Curse on their fawning Arts; from Heav'n it self
I wou'd not, on such Terms, receive a Benefit,
But spurn it back upon the Giver's Hand.

**SELIMA**
My Lord; my Royal Father.
Selima comes forward and kneels to Bajazet.

**BAJAZET**
Ha! what art thou?
What heavenly Innocence? that in a Form
So known, so lov'd, hast left thy Paradise,
For joyless Prison, for this Place of Woe?
Art thou my Selima?

**SELIMA**
Have you forgot me?
Alas! my Piety is then in vain;
Your Selima, your Daughter whom you lov'd,
The Fondling once of her dear Father's Arms,
Is come to claim her share in his Misfortunes;
To wait, and tend him with obsequious Duty;
To sit, and weep for every Care he feels;
To help to wear the tedious Minutes out,
To soften Bondage, and the loss of Empire.

**BAJAZET**

Now by our Prophet! If my wounded Mind
Could know a Thought of Peace, it would be now;
Ev'n from thy prating Infancy thou wert
My Joy, my little Angel; smiling Comfort
Came with thee still to glad me: Now I'm curs'd
Ev'n in thee too; Reproach and Infamy
Attend the Christian Dog, to whom thou wert trusted:
To see thee here!—'twere better see thee dead.

**AXALLA**
Thus Tamerlane, to Royal Bajazet,
With Kingly Greeting sends: Since with the brave,
(The bloody Bus'ness of the Fight once ended)
Stern Hate, and Opposition ought to cease;
Thy Queen already to thy Arms restor'd,
Receive this second Gift, thy beauteous Daughter:
And if there be ought farther in thy Wish,
Demand with Honour, and obtain it freely.

**BAJAZET**
Bear back thy fulsom Greeting to thy Master,
Tell him, I'll none on't: Had he been a God,
All his Omnipotence could not restore
My Fame diminish'd, loss of Sacred Honour,
The Radiancy of Majesty eclips'd.
For ought besides, it is not worth my Care;
The Giver, and his Gifts are both beneath me.

**AXALLA**
Enough of War the wounded Earth has known;
Weary at length, and wasted with Destruction,
Sadly she rears her ruin'd Head, to shew
Her Cities humbled, and her Countries spoil'd,
And to her mighty Masters sues for Peace.
Oh! Sultan! by the Pow'r Divine I swear!
With Joy I wou'd resign the Savage Trophies
In Blood and Battle gain'd, could I attone
The fatal Breach 'twixt thee and Tamerlane;
And think a Soldier's Glory well bestow'd,
To buy Mankind a Peace.

**BAJAZET**
And what art thou?
That dost presume to mediate 'twixt the Rage
Of angry Kings?

**AXALLA**
A Prince, born of the noblest,

And of a Soul that answers to that Birth,
That dares not but do well. Thou dost put on
A forc'd Forgetfulness, thus not to know me,
A Guest so lately to thy Court, then meeting
On gentler Terms.—

**SELIMA**
Could ought efface the Merit
Of brave Axalla's Name, yet when your Daughter
Shall tell, how well, how nobly she was us'd;
How light this gallant Prince made all her Bondage;
Most sure the Royal Bajazet will own,
That Honour stands indebted to such Goodness,
Nor can a Monarch's Friendship more than pay it.

**BAJAZET**
Ha! Know'st thou that fond Girl?—Go—'tis not well—
And when thou cou'd'st descend to take a Benefit
From a vile Christian, and thy Father's Foe,
Thou didst an Act dishonest to thy Race;
Henceforth, unless thou mean'st to cancel all
My Share in thee, and write thy self a Bastard:
Die, Starve, know any Evil, any Pain,
Rather than taste a Mercy from these Dogs.

**SELIMA** [Weeping]
Alas! Axalla!

**AXALLA**
Weep not lovely Maid;
I swear, one pearly Drop from those fair Eyes
Would over pay the Service of my Life;
One Sigh from thee has made a large amends
For all thy angry Father's Frowns, and Fierceness.

**BAJAZET**
Oh! my curs'd Fortune!—am I fall'n thus low?
Dishonour'd to my Face? thou Earth-born thing,
Thou Clod! how hast thou dar'd to lift thy Eyes
Up to the Sacred Race of mighty Ottoman?
Whom Kings, whom ev'n our Prophet's holy Offspring
At distance have beheld; and what art thou?
What glorious Titles blazon out thy Birth?
Thou vile Obscurity! Ha!—say—thou base one.

**AXALLA**
Thus challeng'd Virtue, modest as she is,
Stands up to do her self a common Justice,

To answer, and assert that inborn Merit,
That Worth, which conscious to her self she feels.
Were Honour to be scan'd by long Descent,
From Ancestors Illustrious, I could vaunt
A Lineage of the greatest, and recount
Among my Fathers, Names of antient Story,
Heroes, and God-like Patriots, who subdu'd
The World by Arms, and Virtue, and being Romans
Scorn'd to be Kings; but that be their own Praise:
Nor will I borrow Merit from the Dead,
My self an Undeserver. I could prove
My Friendship such, as thou might'st deign t' accept
With Honour, when it comes with friendly Office,
To render back thy Crown, and former Greatness:
And yet ev'n this, ev'n all is poor, when Selima
With matchless Worth weighs down the adverse Scale.

**BAJAZET**
To give me back what yesterday took from me,
Wou'd be to give like Heav'n, when having finish'd
This World, (the goodly Work of his Creation)
He bid his Favorite, Man, be Lord of all.
But this—

**AXALLA**
Nor is this Gift beyond my Power;
Oft has the mighty Master of my Arms
Urg'd me, with large Ambition to demand
Crowns and Dominions from his bounteous Pow'r:
'Tis true, I wav'd the Proffer, and have held it
The worthier Choice, to wait upon his Virtues,
To be the Friend and Partner of his Wars,
Than to be Asia's Lord: Nor wonder then,
If, in the Confidence of such a Friendship,
I promise boldly for the Royal Giver,
Thy Crown, and Empire.

**BAJAZET**
For our Daughter thus
Mean'st thou to barter? ha! I tell thee, Christian,
There is but one, one Dowry, thou canst give,
And I can ask, worthy my Daughter's Love.

**AXALLA**
Oh! name the mighty Ransom, task my Power,
Let there be Danger, Difficulty, Death,
T' enhance the Price.

**BAJAZET**
I take thee at thy Word,
Bring me the Tartar's Head.

**AXALLA**
Ha!

**BAJAZET**
Tamerlane's,
That Death, that deadly Poison to my Glory.

**AXALLA**
Prodigious! Horrid!

**SELIMA**
Lost! for ever lost!

**BAJAZET**
And could'st thou hope to bribe me with ought else?
With a vile Peace patch'd up on slavish Terms?
With tributary Kingship?—No—to merit
A Recompence from me, sate my Revenge.
The Tartar is my Bane, I cannot bear him;
One Heav'n and Earth can never hold us both;
Still shall we hate, and with Defiance deadly
Keep Rage alive, till one be lost for ever;
As if two Suns should meet in the Meridian,
And strive in fiery Combat for the passage.
Weep'st thou fond Girl? Now as thy King, and Father,
I charge thee, drive this Slave from thy remembrance:
Hate shall be pious in thee;

[Laying hold on her Hand.

—come, and join
To curse thy Father's Foes.

**SELIMA**
Undone for ever!
Now Tyrant Duty, art thou yet obey'd,
There is no more to give thee, Oh Axalla!

[**BAJAZET** leads out **SELIMA**, she looking back on **AXALLA**.

**AXALLA**
'Tis what I fear'd, Fool that I was t'obey:
The Coward Love, that could not bear her Frown,
Has wrought his own Undoing, Perhaps, ev'n now,

The Tyrant's Rage prevails upon her Fears.
She storms, she weeps, and sighs, and trembles,
But swears at length, to think on me no more.
He bad me take her.—But oh! gracious Honour!
Upon what Terms? My Soul yet shudders at it,
And stands, but half recover'd of her Fright.
The Head of Tamerlane! monstrous Impiety!
Bleed, bleed to Death, my Heart, be Virtue's Martyr.
Oh, Emperor, I own I ought to give thee
Some nobler Mark, than Dying, of my Faith.
Then let the Pains I feel my Friendship prove,
'Tis easier far to die, than cease to love.

[Exit **AXALLA**.


SCENE II

Tamerlane's Camp

Enter severally **MONESES**, and **PRINCE of TANAIS**.

**MONESES**
If I not press untimely on his Leisure,
You would much bind a Stranger to your Service,
To give me means of Audience from the Emperor.

**PRINCE of TANAIS**
Most willingly, tho' for the present Moment
We must entreat your stay; he holds him private.

**MONESES**
His Council, I presume,—

**PRINCE of TANAIS**
No; the Affair
Is not of Earth, but Heav'n—a Holy Man,
(One whom our Prophet's Law calls such) a Dervise
Keeps him in Conference.

**MONESES**
Hours of Religion,
Especially of Prince's, claim a Reverence,
Nor will be interrupted.

**PRINCE of TANAIS**
What his Business

Imports, we know not; but with earnest Sute
This Morn he begg'd Admittance. Our great Master
(Than whom none bows more lowly to high Heaven)
In reverend regard holds all that bear
Relation to Religion, and, on notice
Of his Request, receiv'd him on the instant.

**MONESES**
We will attend his Pleasure.

[Exeunt.

[Enter **TAMERLANE**, and a **DERVISE**.

**TAMERLANE**
Thou bring'st me thy Credentials from the Highest,
From Alha, and our Prophet: Speak thy Message,
It must import the best and noblest Ends.

**DERVISE**
Thus speaks our Holy Mahomet, who has giv'n thee
To reign, and conquer; Ill dost thou repay
The Bounties of his Hand, unmindful of
The Fountain, whence thy Streams of Greatness flow,
Thou hast forgot high Heav'n, hast beaten down,
And trampled on Religion's Sanctity.

**TAMERLANE**
Now, as I am a Soldier, and a King,
(The greatest Names of Honour) do but make
Thy Imputation out, and Tamerlane
Shall do thee ample Justice on himself;
So much the Sacred Name of Heav'n awes me.
Cou'd I suspect my Soul of harbouring ought
To its Dishonour, I would search it strictly,
And drive th' offending Thought with Fury forth.

**DERVISE**
Yes, thou hast hurt our Holy Prophet's Honour,
By fostering the pernicious Christian Sect;
Those, whom his Sword pursu'd with fell Destruction,
Thou tak'st into thy Bosom, to thy Councils;
They are thy only Friends: The true Believers
Mourn to behold thee favour this Axalla.

**TAMERLANE**
I fear me, thou out-go'st the Prophet's Order:
And brings his venerable Name, to shelter

A Rudeness ill becoming thee to use,
Or me to suffer. When thou nam'st my Friend,
Thou nam'st a Man beyond a Monk's discerning,
Virtuous, and Great, a Warrior, and a Prince.

**DERVISE**
He is a Christian; there our Law condemns him,
Altho' he were ev'n all thou speak'st, and more.

**TAMERLANE**
'Tis false; no Law Divine condemns the Virtuous,
For differing from the Rules your Schools devise.
Look round, how Providence bestows alike
Sunshine and Rain, to bless the fruitful Year,
On different Nations, all of different Faiths;
And (tho' by several Names and Titles worshipp'd)
Heav'n takes the various Tribute of their Praise;
Since all agree to own, at least to mean,
One best, one greatest, only Lord of All.
Thus when he view'd the many Forms of Nature,
He found that all was good, and blest the fair Variety

**DERVISE**
Most Impious, and Profane!—nay, frown not, Prince,
Full of the Prophet, I despise the Danger
Thy angry Power may threaten: I command thee
To hear, and to obey, since thus says Mahomet;
Why have I made thee dreadful to the Nations?
Why have I giv'n thee Conquest? but to spread
My sacred Law ev'n to the utmost Earth,
And make my Holy Mecca the World's Worship?
Go on, and wheresoe'er thy Arms shall prosper,
Plant there the Prophet's Name: with Sword and Fire,
Drive out all other Faiths, and let the World
Confess him only.

**TAMERLANE**
Had he but commanded
My Sword to conquer all, to make the World
Know but one Lord, the Task were not so hard;
'Twere but to do what has been done already;
And Philip's Son, and Caesar did as much:
But to subdue th' unconquerable Mind,
To make one Reason have the same Effect
Upon all Apprehensions; to force this,
Or this Man, just to think, as thou and I do;
Impossible! Unless Souls were alike
In all, which differ now like Human Faces.

**DERVISE**
Well might the Holy Cause be carry'd on,
If Mussulmen did not make War on Mussulmen.
Why hold'st thou Captive a believing Monarch?
Now, as thou hop'st to 'scape the Prophet's Curse,
Release the Royal Bajazet, and join
With Force united, to destroy the Christians.

**TAMERLANE**
'Tis well—I've found the Cause that mov'd thy Zeal.
What shallow Politician set thee on,
In hopes to fright me this way to compliance?

**DERVISE**
Our Prophet only.—

**TAMERLANE**
No—thou dost belie him,
Thou Maker of new Faiths! that dar'st to build
Thy fond Invensions on Religion's Name.
Religion's Lustre is by [.....] Innocence
Divinely pure, and simple from all Arts.
You daub and dress her like a common Mistress,
The Harlot of your Fancies, and by
False Beauties, which she wants not, makes the World
Suspect, her Angel's Face is foul beneath,
And wo' not bear all Lights. Hence! I have found thee.

**DERVISE**
I have but one resort. Now aid me, Prophet.
[Aside]
Yet have I somewhat further to unfold;
Our Prophet speaks to thee in Thunder—

[The **DERVISE** draws a conceal'd Dagger, and offers to stab **TAMERLANE**.

—thus—

**TAMERLANE**
No, Villain, Heav'n is watchful o'er its Worshippers,

[Wresting the Dagger from him.

And blasts the Murderer's Purpose. Think thou, Wretch,
Think on the Pains that wait thy Crime, and tremble
When I shall doom thee—

**DERVISE**
'Tis but Death at last,
And I will suffer greatly for the Cause
That urg'd me first to the bold Deed.

**TAMERLANE**
Oh, impious!
Enthusiasm thus makes Villains, Martyrs.

[Pausing.

It shall be so.—To die! 'twere a Reward—
Now learn the difference 'twixt thy Faith and mine:
Thine bids thee lift thy Dagger to my Throat,
Mine can forgive the Wrong, and bid thee live.
Keep thy own wicked Secret and be safe:
If thou continu'st still to be the same,
'Tis Punishment enough to be a Villain:
If thou repent'st, I have gain'd one to Virtue,
And am, in that, rewarded for my Mercy.
Hence! from my Sight!—It shocks my Soul, to think
That there is such a Monster in my Kind.

[Exit **DERVISE**.

Whither will Man's Impiety extend?
Oh gracious Heav'n! do'st thou with-hold thy Thunder,
When bold Assassines take thy Name upon 'em,
And swear, they are the Champions of thy Cause?

[Enter **MONESES**.

**MONESES**
Oh, Emperor! before whose awsul Throne

[Kneeling to **TAMERLANE**.
Th' asslicted never kneel in vain for Justice,
Undone, and ruin'd, blasted in my Hopes,
Here let me fall before your sacred Feet,
And groan out my Misfortunes, till your Pity,
(The last Support and Refuge that is left me)
Shall raise me from the Ground, and bid me live.

**TAMERLANE**
Rise, Prince, nor let me reckon up thy Worth,
And tell, how boldly That might bid thee ask,
Lest I should make a Merit of my Justice,
The common Debt I owe to thee, to All,

Ev'n to the meanest of Mankind, the Charter
By which I claim my Crown, and Heav'ns Protection:
Speak then as to a King, the Sacred Name
Where Pow'r is lodg'd, for Righteous Ends alone.

**MONESES**
One only Joy, one Blessing, my fond Heart
Had fix'd its Wishes on, and that is lost;
That Sister, for whose safety my sad Soul
Endur'd a thousand Fears.—

**TAMERLANE**
I well remember,
When e're the Battles join'd, I saw thee first,
With Grief uncommon to a Brother's Love,
Thou told'st a moving Tale of her Misfortunes,
Such as bespoke my Pity. Is there ought
Thou canst demand from Friendship? ask, and have it.

**MONESES**
First, Oh! let me entreat your Royal Goodness.
Forgive the Folly of a Lover's Caution,
That forg'd a Tale of Falshood to deceive you:
Said I, she was my Sister?—Oh! 'tis false,
She holds a dearer Interest in my Soul,
Such as the closest ties of Blood ne'er knew:
An Int'rest, such as Pow'r, Wealth and Honour
Can't buy, but Love, Love only can bestow;
She was the Mistress of my Vows, my Bride,
By Contract mine; and long e're this, the Priest
Had ty'd the Knot for ever, had not Bajazet—

**TAMERLANE**
Ha! Bajazet!—If yet his Pow'r with-holds
The Cause of all thy Sorrows, all thy Fears,
Ev'n Gratitude for once shall gain upon him,
Spight of his savage Temper, to restore her.
This Morn a Soldier brought a Captive Beauty,
Sad, tho' she seem'd yet of a Form most rare,
By much the noblest Spoil of all the Field;
Ev'n Scipto, or a Victor yet more cold,
Might have forgot his Virtue, at her light
Struck with a pleasing Wonder, I beheld her
Till by a Slave that waited near her Person,
I learnt she was the Captive Sultan's Wife,
Strait I forbid my Eyes the dangerous Joy
Of gazing long, and sent her to her Lord.

**MONESES**

There was Moneses lost.—Too sure my Heart
(From the first mention of her wond'rous Charms)
Presag'd it cou'd be only my Arpasia.

**TAMERLANE**

Arpasia! didst thou say?

**MONESES**

Yes, my Arpasia.

**TAMERLANE**

Sure I mistake, or fain I would mistake thee.
I nam'd the Queen of Bajazet, his Wife.

**MONESES**

His Queen! His Wife! He brings that Holy Title,
To varnish o'er the monstrous Wrongs he has done me.

**TAMERLANE**

Alas! I fear me, Prince, thy Griefs are just;
Thou art indeed unhappy.—

**MONESES**

Can you pity me,
And not redress?

[Kneeling.

Oh, Royal Tamerlane!
Thou Succour of the Wretched, reach thy Mercy,
To save me from the Grave, and from Oblivion;
Be gracious to the Hopes that wait my Youth.
Oh! let not Sorrow blast me, lest I wither,
And fall in vile Dishonour. Let thy Justice
Restore me my Arpasia; give her back,
Back to my Wishes, to my Transports give her,
To my fond, restless, bleeding, dying Bosom:
Oh! give her to me yet while I have Life
To bless thee for the Bounty. Oh, Arpasia!

**TAMERLANE**

Unhappy Royal Youth, why dost thou ask,
What Honour must deny? Ha! Is she not
His Wife, whom he has wedded, whom enjoy'd?
And would'st thou have my partial Friendship break
That Holy Knot, which ty'd once, all Mankind
Agree to hold Sacred, and Undissolvable?

The Brutal Violence would stain my Justice,
And brand me with a Tyrant's hated Name
To late Posterity.

**MONESES**
Are then the Vows,
The Holy Vows we registred in Heav'n,
But common Air?

**TAMERLANE**
Could thy fond Love forget
The Violation of a first Enjoyment?—
But Sorrow has disturb'd and hurt thy Mind.

**MONESES**
Perhaps it has, and like an idle Madman,
That wanders with a Train of hooting Boys,
I do a thousand things to shame my Reason.
Then let me fly, and bear my Follies with me
Far, far from the World's Sight; Honour, and Fame,
Arms, and the glorious War shall be forgotten:
No noble Sound of Greatn ss, or Ambition,
Shall wake my drowsie Soul from her dead Sleep,
Till the last Trump do summon.

**TAMERLANE**
Let thy Virtue
Stand up, and answer to these warring Passions,
That vex thy manly Temper. From the moment
When first I saw thee, something wondrous noble
Shone thro' thy Form, and won my Friendship for thee,
Without the tedious Form of long Acquaintance;
Nor will I lose thee poorly for a Woman.
Come, droop no more, thou shalt with me pursue
True Greatness, till we rise to Immortality;
Thou shalt forget these lesser Cares, Moneses,
Thou shalt, and help me to reform the World.

**MONESES**
So the good Genius warns his mortal Charge,
To fly the evil Fate, that still pursues him,
Till it have wrought his Ruin. Sacred Tamerlane,
Thy Words are as the Breath of Angels to me:
But oh! too deep the wounding Grief is fixt
For any Hand to heal.

**TAMERLANE**
This dull Despair

Is the Soul's Laziness: Rouse to the Combat,
And thou art sure to conquer. War shall restore thee;
The Sound of Arms shall wake thy martial Ardour,
And cure this amorous Sickness of thy Soul,
Begun by Sloth, and nurs'd by too much Ease;
The idle God of Love supinely dreams,
Amidst inglorious Shades and purling Streams;
In rosie Fetters, and fantastick Chains,
He binds deluded Maids and simple Swains,
With soft Enjoyments, wooes 'em to forget
The hardy Toils, and Labours of the great.
But if the warlike Trumpet's loud Alarms
To virtuous Acts excite, and manly Arms;
The Coward Boy avows his abject Fear,
On silken Wings sublime he cuts the Air,
Scar'd at the noble Noise, and Thunder of the War.

[Exeunt.


ACT IV

SCENE I

SCENE, Bajazet's Tent

Enter **HALY** and the **DERVISE**.


**HALY**
To 'scape with Life from an Attempt like this,
Demands my Wonder justly.


**DERVISE**
True it may;
But 'tis a Principle of his new Faith;
'Tis what his Christian Favorites have inspir'd,
Who fondly make a Merit of Forgiveness,
And give their Foes a second Opportunity,
If the first Blow should miss:—Failing to serve
The Sultan to my wish, and ev'n despairing
Of further means, t' effect his Liberty,
A lucky Accident retriev'd my Hopes.


**HALY**
The Prophet, and our Master will reward
Thy Zeal in their behalf; but speak thy Purpose.

**DERVISE**

Just ent'ring here I met the Tartar General, Fierce Omar.

**HALY**

He commands (if I mistake not)
This Quarter of the Army, and our Guards.

**DERVISE**

The same; by his stern Aspect, and the Fires
That Kindled in his Eyes, I guess'd the Tumult
Some Wrong had rais'd in his tempestuous Soul;
A Friendship of old Date had giv'n me Privilege,
To ask of his Concerns; In short I learn'd,
That burning for the Sultan's beauteous Daughter,
He had beg'd her, as a Captive of the War,
From Tamerlane; but meeting with denial
Of what he thought his Services might claim,
Loudly he storms, and curses the Italian,
As cause of this Affront: I join'd his Rage,
And added to his Injuries, the Wrongs
Our Prophet daily meets from this Axalla.
But see, he comes. Improve what I shall tell,
And all we wish is ours.—
They seem to talk together aside.

[Enter **OMAR**.

**OMAR**

No—if I forgive it,
Dishonour blast my Name; was it for this
That I directed his first Steps to Greatness?
Taught him to climb, and made him what he is?
When our great Cam first bent his Eyes towards him,
(Then petty Prince of Parthia) and by me
Perswaded, rais'd him to his Daughter's Bed,
Call'd him his Son, and Successor of Empire:
Was it for this, that like a Rock I stood,
And stemm'd the Torrent of our Tartar Lords,
Who scorn'd his upstart Sway? When Calibes
In bold Rebellion drew ev'n half the Provinces
To own his Cause, I, like his better Angel,
Stood by his shaking Throne, and fixt it fast;
And am I now so lost to his Remembrance?
That when I ask a Captive he shall tell me,
She is Axalla's Right, his Christian Minion.

**DERVISE**

Allow me, valiant Omar, to demand,

Since injur'd thus, why right you not your self?
The Prize you ask is in your Power.

**OMAR**
It is,
And I will seize it, in despight of Tamerlane,
And that Italian Dog.

**HALY**
What need of Force,
When every thing concurs to meet your Wishes?
Our mighty Master would not wish a Son
Nobler than Omar; from a Father's hand
Receive that Daughter, which ungrateful Tamerlane
Has to your Worth deny'd.

**OMAR**
Now by my Arms,
It will be great Revenge. What will your Sultan
Give to the Man that shall restore his Liberty,
His Crown? and give him Pow'r to wreck his Hatred
Upon his greatest Foe?

**HALY**
All he can ask,
And far beyond his Wish.—

[Trumpets.

**OMAR**
These Trumpets speak
The Emperor's Approach; he comes, once more,
To offer Terms of Peace; retire—within
I will know farther,—he grows deadly to me,
And curse me, Prophet, if I not repay
His Hate, with retribution full as mortal.

[Exeunt.

[Scene draws, discovers **ARPASIA** lying on a Couch.

**A SONG to Sleep. By a Lady.**
Too Thee, oh! gentle Sleep, alone
Is owing all our Peace,
By Thee our Joys are heighten'd shown,
By Thee our Sorrows cease.
The Nymph, whose Hand, by Fraud, or Force,
Some Tyrant has possess'd,

By Thee, obtaining a Divorce,
In her own Choice, is blest.
Oh! stay; Arpasia bids thee stay,
The sadly weeping Fair
Conjures Thee, not to lose in Day
The Object of her Care.
To grasp whose pleasing Form she sought,
That Motion chac'd her Sleep,
Thus by our selves, are oftnest wrought
The Griefs, for which we weep.

**ARPASIA**
Oh! Death! thou gentle end of human Sorrows,
Still must my weary Eye-lids vainly wake
In tedious Expectation of thy Peace:
Why stand thy thousand thousand Doors still open,
To take the Wretched in? if stern Religion
Guards every Passage, and forbids my Entrance?—
Lucrece could bleed, and Porcia swallow Fire,
When urg'd with Griefs beyond a mortal Sufferance;
But here it must not be. Think then, Arpasia,
Think on the Sacred Dictates of thy Faith,
And let that arm thy Virtue, to perform
What Cato's Daughter durst not,—Live Arpasia,
And dare to be unhappy.

[Enter **TAMERLANE**, and **ATTENDANTS**.

**TAMERLANE**
When Fortune smiles upon the Soldier's Arms,
And adds ev'n Beauty to adorn his Conquest,
Yet she ordains, the fair should know no Fears,
No Sorrows, to pollute their lovely Eyes;
But should be us'd ev'n nobly, as her self,
The Queen and Goddess of the Warrior's Vows,—
Such Welcome, as a Camp can give, fair Sultaness,
We hope you have receiv'd; It shall be larger,
And better, as it may.

**ARPASIA**
Since I have born
That miserable Mark of fatal Greatness,
I have forgot all difference of Conditions,
Scepters and Fetters are grown equal to me,
And the best Change, my Fate can bring, is Death.

**TAMERLANE**
When Sorrow dwells in such an Angel Form,

Well may we guess, that those above are Mourners;
Virtue is wrong'd, and bleeding Innocence
Suffers some wond'rous Violation here,
To make the Saints look sad. Oh! teach my Power
To cure those Ills, which you unjustly suffer,
Lest Heav'n should wrest it from my idle Hand,
If I look on, and see you weep in vain.

**ARPASIA**
Not that my Soul disdains the generous Aid,
Thy Royal Goodness proffers; but oh! Emperor,
It is not in my Fate to be made happy:
Nor will I listen to the Cos'ner, Hope;
But stand resolv'd, to bear the beating Storm,
That roars around me; safe in this alone,
That I am not Immortal.—Tho' 'tis hard,
'Tis wond'rous hard, when I remember thee
(Dear Native Greece) and you, ye weeping Maids,
That were Companions of my Virgin Youth:
My noble Parents! Oh! the grief of Heart!
The Pangs, that, for unhappy me, bring down
Their reverend Ages to the Grave with Sorrow:
And yet there is a Woe surpassing all,
Ye Saints and Angels, give me of your Constancy,
If you expect I shall endure it long.

**TAMERLANE**
Why is my Pity all, that I can give
To Tears like yours? And yet I fear 'tis all;
Nor dare I ask, what mighty Loss you mourn,
Lest Honour should forbid to give it back.

**ARPASIA**
No, Tamerlane, nor did I mean thou shoud'st.
But know (tho' to the weakness of my Sex
I yield these Tears) my Soul is more than Man.
Think I am born a Greek, nor doubt my Virtue:
A Greek! from whose fam'd Ancestors of old,
Rome drew the Patterns of her boasted Heroes:
They must be mighty Evils, that can vanquish
A Spartan Courage, and a Christian Faith.

[Enter **BAJAZET**.

**BAJAZET**
To know no thought of Rest! to have the Mind
Still ministring fresh Plagues! as in a Circle,
Where one Dishonour treads upon another;

What know the Fiends beyond it?—

[Seeing **ARPASIA** and **TAMERLANE**.

Ha! by Hell!
There wanted only this, to make me mad.
Comes he to triumph here? to rob my Love?
And violate the last retreat of Happiness?

**TAMERLANE**
But that I read upon thy frowning Brow,
That War yet lives, and rages in thy Breast;
Once more, (in pity to the suff'ring World)
I meant to offer Peace.—

**BAJAZET**
And mean'st Thou too
To treat it with our Empress? and to barter
The Spoils, which Fortune gave thee, for her Favours?

**ARPASIA** [Aside]
What would the Tyrant?—

**BAJAZET**
Seek'st thou thus our Friendship?
Is this the Royal Usage, thou didst boast?

**TAMERLANE**
The boiling Passion that disturbs thy Soul,
Spreads Clouds around, and makes thy Purpose dark.—
Unriddle what thy mystick Fury aims at.

**BAJAZET**
Is it a Riddle?—Read it there explain'd,
There in my Shame. Now judge me thou, O Prophet,
And equal Heav'n, if this demand not Rage!
The Peasant-Hind, begot, and born to Slavery,
Yet dares assert a Husband's sacred Right,
And guard his homely Couch from Violation.
And shall a Monarch tamely bear the Wrong
Without complaining?

**TAMERLANE**
If I could have wrong'd thee,
If conscious Virtue, and all-judging Heav'n
Stood not between, to bar ungovern'd Appetite,
What hinder'd, but in spight of thee, my Captive,
I might have us'd a Victor's boundless Power,

And sated every Wish my Soul could form?
But to secure thy Fears, know, Bajazet,
This is among the Things I dare not do.

**BAJAZET**
By Hell! 'tis false; else, wherefore art thou present?
What cam'st thou for, but to undo my Honour?
I found thee holding amorous Parley with her,
Gazing, and gloting on her wanton Eyes,
And bargaining for Pleasures yet to come;
My Life, I know, is the devoted Price,
But take it, I am weary of the Pain.

**TAMERLANE**
Yet e'er thou rashly urge my Rage too far,
I warn thee to take heed; I am a Man,
And have the Frailties common to Man's Nature;
The fiery Seeds of Wrath are in my Temper,
And may be blown up to so sierce a Blaze,
As Wisdom cannot rule. Know, thou hast toucht me
Ev'n in the nicest, tenderest part, my Honour.
My Honour! which, like Pow'r, disdains being question'd;
Thy Breath has blasted my fair Virtue's Fame,
And mark'd me for a Villain, and a Tyrant

**ARPASIA**
And stand I here an idle Looker on?
To s e my innocence murder'd and mangled
By barbarous Hands? nor can revenge the Wrong
Art thou a Man, and dar'st thou use me thus?
Hast thou not torn me from my Native Country?
From the dear Arms of my many Friends?
From my Soul's Peace, and from my injur'd Love?
Hast thou not ruin'd, blotted me for ever,
And driv'n me to the brink of black Despair?
And is it in thy Malice yet, to add
A Wound more deep, to sully my white Name,
My Virtue?—

**BAJAZET**
Yes, thou hast thy Sexes Virtues,
Their Affectation, Pride, Ill Nature, Noise,
Proneness to change, ev'n from the Joy that pleas'd 'em:
So gracious is your Idol, dear Variety,
That for another Love you would forego
An Angel's Form, to mingle with a Devil's;
Through every State, and Rank of Men you wander;
Till ev'n your large Experience takes in all

The different Nations of the Peopled Earth.

**ARPASIA**
Why sought'st thou not from thy own Impious Tribe
A Wife, like one of these? for such thy Race
(If human Nature brings forth such) affords.
Greece, for chaste Virgins fam'd, and pious Matrons,
Teems not with Monsters, like your Turkish Wives;
Whom guardian Eunuchs, haggard and deform'd,
Whom Walls and Bars make honest by constraint.
Know, I detest, like Hell, the Crime thou mention'st:
Not that I fear, or reverence thee, thou Tyrant:
But that my Soul, conscious of whence it sprung,
Sits unpolluted in its sacred Temple,
And scorns to mingle with a Thought so mean.

**TAMERLANE**
Oh Pity! that a Greatness so divine
Should meet a Fate so wretched, so unequal.—
Thou blind and wilful, to the Good that courts thee;
[To **BAJAZET**.
With open-handed Bounty Heav'n pursues thee,
And bids thee (undeserving as thou art,
And monstrous in thy Crimes) be happy yet:
Whilst thou, in Fury, do'st avert the Blessings,
And art an evil Genius to thy self.

**BAJAZET**
No—Thou! thou art my greatest Curse on Earth.
Thou, who hast robb'd me of my Crown and Glory,
And now pursu'st me to the Verge of Life,
To spoil me of my Honour. Thou! thou Hypocrite!
That wear'st a Pageant out-side shew of Virtue,
To cover the hot Thoughts, that glow within,
Thou rank Adulterer!

**TAMERLANE**
Oh! That thou wert
The Lord of all those Thousands, that lie breathless
On yonder Field of Blood: That I again
Might hunt thee in the Face of Death and Danger,
Through the tumultuous Battle, and there force thee,
Vanquish'd and sinking underneath my Arm,
To own, thou hast traduc'd me, like a Villain.

**BAJAZET**
Ha! does it gall thee, Tartar? By Revenge?
It joys me much, to find, thou feel'st my Fury.

Yes! I will Eccho to thee, thou Adulterer!
Thou dost profane the Name of King and Soldier,
And like a Ruffian-Bravo cam'st with Force
To violate the Holy Marriage-Bed.

**TAMERLANE**
Wer't thou not shelter'd by thy abject State,
The Captive of my Sword, by my just Anger!
My Breath, like Thunder, should confound thy Pride,
And doom thee dead, this instant, with a Word.

**BAJAZET**
'Tis false! my Fate's above thee, and thou dar'st not.

**TAMERLANE**
Ha! dare not? Thou hast rais'd my pond'rous Rage,
And now it falls to crush thee at a Blow.
A Guard there.—

[Enter a **GUARD**, they seize **BAJAZET**.

Seize and drag him to his Fate.
Tyrant, I'll do a double Justice on thee,
At once revenge my self, and all Mankind.

**BAJAZET**
Well do'st thou, e'er thy Violence and Lust
Invade my Bed, thus to begin with Murder;
Drown all thy Fears in Blood, and sin securely.

**TAMERLANE**
Away!—

**ARPASIA** [Kneeling]
Oh stay! I charge thee, by Renown,
By that bright Glory, thy great Soul pursues!
Call back the Doom of Death.

**TAMERLANE**
Fair injur'd Excellence,
Why dost thou kneel, and waste such precious Pray'rs,
(As might ev'n bribe the Saints to partial Justice)
For one to Goodness lost? who first undid thee,
Who still pursues, and aggravates the Wrong.

**BAJAZET**
By Alha! no—I will not wear a Life
Bought with such vile Dishonour.—Death shall free me

At once from Infamy, and thee, thou Traytress!

**ARPASIA**
No matter, tho' the whistling Winds grow loud,
And the rude Tempest roars, 'tis idle Rage,
Oh! mark it not. But let thy steady Virtue
Be constant to its Temper; save his Life,
And save Arpasia from the sport of Talkers.
Think, how the busie, medling World shall toss
Thy mighty Name about, in scurril Mirth;
Shall brand thy Vengeance, as a foul Design,
And make such monstrous Legends of our Lives,
As late Posterity shall blush in reading.

**TAMERLANE**
Oh matchless Virtue! Yes I will obey;
Tho' Laggard in the Race, admiring yet,
I will pursue the shining Path thou tread'st.
Sultan, be safe. Reason resumes her Empire,

[The **GUARDS** release **BAJAZET**.

And I am cool again.—Here break we off,
Lest further Speech should minister new Rage.
Wisely from dangerous Passions I retreat,
To keep a Conquest, which was hard to get:
And oh! 'tis time I shou'd for Flight prepare,
A War more fatal seems to threaten there,
And all my Rebel-blood assists the Fair:
One moment more, and I too late shall find,
That Love's the strongest Pow'r that lords it o'er the Mind.

[Exit **TAMERLANE** followed by the **GUARDS**.

**BAJAZET**
To what new Shame, what Plague am I reserv'd?
Why did my Stars refuse me to die warm?
While yet my Regal State stood unimpeach'd,
Nor knew the Curse of having One above me;
Then too (altho' by force I graspt the Joy)
My Love was safe, nor felt the rack of doubt:
Why hast thou forc'd this nauseous Life upon me?
Is it to triumph over me?—But I will,
I will be free, I will forget thee all;
The Bitter and the Sweet, the Joy and Pain,
Death shall expunge at once, and ease my Soul.
Prophet, take notice, I disclaim thy Paradice,
Thy fragrant Bow'rs, and everlasting Shades,

Thou hast plac'd Woman there, and all thy Joys are tainted.

[Exit **BAJAZET**.

**ARPASIA**
A little longer yet, be strong, my Heart,
A little longer let the busie Spirits
Keep on their chearful round.—It wo' not be:
Love, Sorrow, and the Sting of vile Reproach,
Succeeding one another in their Course,
Like Drops of eating Water on the Marble,
At length have worn my boasted Courage down:
I will indulge the Woman in my Soul,
And give a loose to Tears, and to Impatience;
Death is at last my due, and I will have it.—
And see, the poor Moneses comes to take
One sad Adieu, and then we part for ever.

[Enter **MONESES**.

**MONESES**
Already am I onward of my way;
Thy tuneful Voice comes like a hollow Sound
At distance to my Ears. My Eyes grow heavy,
And all the glorious Lights of Heav'n look dim;
'Tis the last Office they shall ever do me,
To view thee once, and then to close and die.

**ARPASIA**
Alas! how happy have we been, Moneses?
Yee gentle Days, that once were ours; what Joys
Did every chearful Morning bring along?
No Fears, no Jealousies, no angry Parents,
That for unequal Births, or Fortunes frown'd;
But Love, that kindly join'd our Hearts, to bless us,
Made us a Blessing too to all besides.

**MONESES**
Oh! Cast not thy remembrance back, Arpasia,
'Tis Grief unutterable, 'tis Distraction!
But let this last of hours be peaceful Sorrow;
Here let me kneel, and pay my latest Vows;
Be witness, all ye Saints, thou Heav'n and Nature,
Be witness of my Truth, for you have known it;
Be witness, that I never knew a Pleasure,
In all the World cou'd offer, like Arpasia;
Be witness, that I liv'd but in Arpasia;
And oh! be witness, that her Loss has kill'd me.

**ARPASIA**

While thou art speaking, Life begins to fail,
And every tender Accent chills like Death.
Oh! let me haste then yet, e'er Day declines,
And the long Night prevail, once more, to tell thee
What, and how dear Moneses has been to me.
What has he not been?—All the Names of Love,
Brothers, or Fathers, Husbands, all are poor:
Moneses is my self, in my fond Heart,
Ev'n in my vital Blood he lives and reigns;
The last dear Object of my parting Soul
Will be Moneses; the last Breath that lingers
Within my panting Breast, shall sigh Moneses.

**MONESES**

It is enough! Now to thy Rest, my Soul,
The World, and thou have made an end at once.

**ARPASIA**

Fain would I still detain thee, hold thee still;
Nor Honour can forbid, that we together
Should share the poor few Minutes that remain;
I swear, methinks this sad Society
Has somewhat pleasing in it.—Death's dark Shades
Seem, as we Journy on, to lose their Horror:
At near approach the Monsters form'd by Fear
Are vanisht all, and leave the Prospect clear:
Amidst the gloomy Vale, a pleasing Scene
With Flow'rs adorn'd, and never-fading Green,
Inviting stands to take the Wretched in.
No Wars, no Wrongs, no Tyrants, no Despair,
Disturb the Quiet of a Place so fair,
But injur'd Lovers find Elizium there.

[Exeunt.

[Enter **BAJAZET**, **OMAR**, **HALY**, and the **DERVISE**.

**BAJAZET**

Now by the glorious Tomb, that shrines our Prophet,
By Mecca's sacred Temple! here I swear!
Our Daughter is thy Bride; and to that Gift
Such Wealth, such Pow'r, such Honours will I add,
That Monarchs shall with Envy view thy State,
And own, Thou art a Demy-God to them.
Thou hast giv'n me what I wish'd, Power of Revenge,
And when a King rewards, 'tis ample Retribution.

**OMAR**
Twelve Tartar Lords, each potent in his Tribe,
Have sworn to own my Cause, and draw their Thousands
To Morrow, from th' ungrateful Parthian's side;
The Day declining seems to yield to Night,
E'er little more than half her Course be ended,
In an auspicious Hour prepare for Flight;
The Leaders of the Troops thro' which we pass,
Rais'd by my Pow'r, devoted to my Service,
Shall make our Passage secret, and secure.

**DERVISE**
Already, mighty Sultan, art thou safe,
Since by yon passing Torches Light, I guess
To his Pavilion Tamerlane retires,
Attended by a Train of waiting Courtiers.
All, who remain within these Tents, are thine,
And hail thee, as their Lord.
Ha, th' Italian Prince,
With sad Moneses are not yet gone forth.

**BAJAZET**
Ha! With our Queen and Daughter?

**OMAR**
They are ours;
I markt the Slaves, who waited on Axalla;
They, when the Emperor past out, prest on,
And mingled with the Crowd, nor mist their Lord:
He is your Pris'ner, Sir, I go this moment,
To seize, and bring him, to receive his Doom.

[Exit **OMAR**.

**BAJAZET**
Haste, Haly, follow, and secure the Greek,
Him too I wish to keep within my Power.

[Exit **HALY**.

**DERVISE**
If my dread Lord permit his Slave to speak,
I would advise to spare Axalla's Life,
Till we are safe beyond the Parthian's Power:
Him, as our Pledge of Safety, may we hold;
And, could you gain him to assist your Flight,
It might import you much.

**BAJAZET**
Thou Counsell'st well;
And tho' I hate him, for he is a Christian,
And to my mortal Enemy devoted,
Yet to secure my Liberty, and Vengeance,
I wish he now were ours.

**DERVISE**
And see! they come!
Fortune repents, again she courts your Side,
And, with this first fair Offering of Success,
She wooes you, to forget her Crime of yesterday.

[Enter **OMAR** with **AXALLA** Prisoner, **SELIMA** following weeping.

**AXALLA**
I wo'not call thee Villain, 'tis a Name
Too holy for thy Crime; to break thy Faith,
And turn a Rebel to so good a Master,
Is an Ingratitude unmatch'd on Earth;
The first revolting Angel's Pride cou'd only
Do more, than thou hast done. Thou Copy'st well,
And keep'st the black Original in view.

**OMAR**
Do, Rage, and vainly call upon thy Master,
To save his Minion; my Revenge has caught thee,
And I will make thee curse that fond Presumption,
That set thee on, to rival me in ought.

**BAJAZET**
Christian, I hold thy Fate at my Disposal.
One only way remains to Mercy open,
Be Partner of my Flight, and my Revenge,
And thou art safe. Thy other Choice is Death.

**OMAR**
What means the Sultan?

**DERVISE**
I Conjure you, hold—
Your Rival is devoted to Destruction,
[Aside to **OMAR**]
Nor would the Sultan now defer his Fate
But for our common safety—
[Whispers]
Listen further.

**AXALLA**

Then briefly thus. Death is the Choice, I make;
Since, next to Heav'n, my Master, and my Friend
Has Interest in my Life, and still shall claim it.

**BAJAZET**

Then take thy Wish.—Call in our Mutes.

**SELIMA**

My Father,
If yet you have not sworn to cast me off,
And turn me out, to wander in Misfortune;
If yet my Voice be gracious in your Ears;
If yet my Duty and my Love offend not,
Oh! call your Sentence back, and save Axalla.

**BAJAZET**

Rise, Selima, the Slave deserves to die,
Who durst, with sullen Pride, refuse my Mercy:
Yet, for thy sake, once more I offer Life.

**SELIMA**

Some Angel whisper to my anxious Soul
What I shall do to save him.—Oh! Axalla!
Is it so easie to thee, to sorsake me?
Can'st thou resolve, with all this cold Indifference,
Never to see me more? To leave me here
The miserable Mourner of thy Fate,
Condemn'd, to waste my Widow'd Virgin Youth,
My tedious Days and Nights in lonely Weeping,
And never know the Voice of Comfort more.

**AXALLA**

Search not too deep the Sorrows of my Breast;
Thou say'st, I am Indifferent, and Cold.
Oh! is it possible, my Eyes should tell
So little of the fighting Storm within.
Oh! turn thee from me, save me from thy Beauties,
Falshood and Ruin all look lovely there.
Oh! let my lab'ring Soul yet struggle thro'—
I will—I would resolve to die, and leave thee.

**BAJAZET**

Then let him die.—He trifles with my Favour;
I have too long attended his Resolves.

**SELIMA** [To **BAJAZET**]

Oh! stay a Minute, yet a Minute longer;
A Minute is a little space in Life:
There is a kind Consenting in his Eyes,
And I shall win him to your Royal Will.
Oh! my Axalla, seem but to consent—
[To **AXALLA** aside]
Unkind and Cruel, will you then do nothing?
I find, I am not worth thy least of Cares.

**AXALLA**
Oh! labour not to hang Dishonour on me:
I could bear Sickness, Pain, and Poverty,
Those mortal Evils worse than Death, for thee.
But this.—It has the force of Fate against us,
And cannot be.

**SELIMA**
See, see, Sir, he relents,
[To **BAJAZET**]
Already he inclines to own your Cause:
A little longer, and he is all yours.

**BAJAZET**
Then mark how far a Father's Fondness yields:
Till Midnight I defer the Death he merits,
And give him up till then to thy Persuasion.
If by that time he meets my Will, he lives;
If not, thy self shalt own, he dies with Justice.

**AXALLA**
'Tis but to lengthen Life upon the Rack.
I am resolv'd already.

**SELIMA**
Oh! be still,
Nor rashly urge a Ruin on us both,
'Tis but a moment more I have to save thee
Be kind, auspicious Alha, to my Pray'r,
More for my Love, than for my Self I fear,
Neglect Mankind awhile, and make him all thy Care.

[Exeunt **AXALLA** and **SELIMA**.

**BAJAZET**
Moneses!—Is that Dog secur'd?

**OMAR**
He is.

**BAJAZET**
'Tis well—My Soul perceives returning Greatness,
As Nature feels the Spring. Lightly she bounds,
And shakes Dishonour, like a Burden, from her,
Once more Imperial, awful, and her self.
So when of old Jove from the Titans fled,
Ammon's rude Front his radiant Face bely'd,
And all the Majesty of Heaven lay hid.
At length by Fate to Pow'r Divine restor'd,
His Thunder taught the World, to know its Lord,
The God grew terrible again, and was again ador'd.

[Exeunt.


ACT V

SCENE I

SCENE, Bajazet's Tent

Enter **ARPASIA**.

**ARPASIA**
Sure 'tis a Horror, more than Darkness brings,
That sits upon the Night; Fate is abroad.
Some ruling Fiend hangs in the dusky Air,
And scatters Ruin, Death, and wild Distraction,
O'er all the wretched Race of Man below:
Not long ago, a Troop of ghastly Slaves
Rush'd in, and forc'd Moneses from my Sight;
Death hung so heavy on his drooping Spirits,
That scarcely could he say—Farewel—for ever.
And yet, methinks, some gentle Spirit whispers
Thy Peace draws near, Arpasia, sigh no more;
And see the King of Terrors is at hand;
His Minister appears.

[Enter **BAJAZET**, and **HALY**.

**BAJAZET** [Aside to **HALY**]
The rest I leave
To thy dispatch. For oh! my faithful Haly,
Another Care has taken up thy Master;
Spight of the high-wrought Tempest in my Soul,
Spight of the Pangs, which Jealousie has cost me;

This haughty Woman reigns within my Breast:
In vain I strive to put her from my Thoughts,
To drive her out with Empire, and Revenge:
Still she comes back like a retiring Tide,
Still she comes back like a retiring Tide,
That Ebbs a while, but strait returns again,
And swells above the Beach.

**HALY**
Why wears my Lord
An anxious Thought, for what his Pow'r commands?
When in an happy Hour, you shall e'er long
Have born the Empress, from amidst your Foes,
She must be yours, be only, and all yours.

**BAJAZET**
On that depends my Fear. Yes! I must have her,
I own I will not, cannot go without her;
But such is the Condition of our Flight,
That shou'd she not consent, 'twould hazard all,
To bear her hence by force; Thus I resolve then,
By Threats, and Pray'rs, by ev'ry way to move her;
If all prevail not, Force is left, at last;
And I will set Life, Empire on the Venture,
To keep her mine.—Be near, to wait my Will.

[Exit **HALY**.

When last we parted, 'twas on angry Terms,
Let the remembrance die, or kindly think
That jealous Rage is but a hasty Flame,
That blazes out, when Love too siercely burns.

**ARPASIA**
For thee to wrong me, and for me to suffer,
Is the hard Lesson that my Soul has learnt;
And now I stand prepar'd for all to come:
Nor is it worth my leisure to distinguish,
If Love, or Jealousie commit the violence;
Each have alike been fatal to my Peace,
Confirming me a Wretch, and thee a Tyrant.

**BAJAZET**
Still to deform thy gentle Brow with Frowns!
And still to be perverse! It is a manner
Abhorrent from the softness of thy Sex:
Women, like Summer Storms, a while are Cloudy,
Burst out in Thunder, and impetuous Show'rs;

But strait the Sun of Beauty dawns abroad,
And all the fair Horizon is serene.

**ARPASIA**
Then to retrieve the Honour of my Sex,
Here I disclaim that Changing, and Inconstancy;
To Thee I will be ever, as I am.

**BAJAZET**
Thou say'st, I am a Tyrant, think so still,
And let it warn thy Prudence, to lay hold
On the good Hour of Peace, that courts thee now;
Souls form'd like mine, brook being scorn'd, but ill;
Be well advis'd, and profit by my Patience,
It is a short-liv'd Virtue.

**ARPASIA**
Turn thy Eyes
Back on the Story of my Woes, Barbarian.
Thou that hast violated all Respects
Due to my Sex, and Honour of my Birth,
Thou brutal Ravisher! that hast undone me,
Ruin'd my Love! Can I have Peace with thee?
Impossible! first Heav'n and Hell shall join,
They only differ more.

**BAJAZET**
I see, 'tis vain,
To court thy stubborn Temper with Endearments.
Resolve this moment, to return my Love,
And be the willing Partner of my Flight,
Or by the Prophet's holy Law! thou dy'st.

**ARPASIA**
And dost thou hope, to fright me with that Fantome?
Death! 'Tis the greatest Mercy thou can'st give;
So frequent are the Murders of thy Reign,
One Day scarce passing by unmark'd with Blood,
That Children, by long use, have learnt to scorn it:
Know, I disdain to aid thy treach'rous purpose,
And shou'dst thou dare to force me, with my Cries
I will call Heav'n and Earth to my Assistance.

**BAJAZET**
Confusion! dost thou brave me? But my Wrath
Shall find a Passage to thy swelling Heart,
And rack thee worse, than all the Pains of Death.
That Grecian Dog, the Minion of thy Wishes,

Shall be dragg'd forth, and butcher'd in thy sight;
Thou shalt behold him, when his Pangs are terrible,
Then, when he stares, and gasps, and struggles strongly,
Ev'n in the bitterest Agony of dying;
'Till thou shalt rend thy Hair, tear out thy Eyes,
And curse thy Pride, while I applaud my Vengeance.

**ARPASIA**
Oh! satal Image! All my Pow'rs give way,
And Resolution sickens at the Thought;
A Flood of Passion rises in my Breast,
And labours fiercely upward to my Eyes.
Come, all ye great Examples of my Sex,

**ARPASIA**
Of somthing soft,
Tender and kind, of somthing wond'rous sad.
Oh! my full Soul!

**MONESES**
My Tongue is at a loss,
Thoughts crowd so fast, thy Name is all I've left,
My kindest! truest! dearest! best Arpasia!

[The **MUTES** struggle with him.

**ARPASIA**
I have a thousand, thousand Things to utter,
A thousand more to hear yet. Barbarous Villains!
Give me a Minute. Speak to me, Moneses.

**MONESES**
Speak to thee? 'Tis the Business of my Life,
'Tis all the use I have for vital Air.
Stand off ye Slaves! To tell thee, that my Heart
Is full of thee; that ev'n at this dread moment
My fond Eyes gaze with Joy and Rapture on thee,
Angels and Light it self are not so fair.

[Enter **BAJAZET**, **HALY**, and **ATTENDANTS**.

**BAJAZET**
Ha! wherefore lives this Dog? Be quick, ye Slaves,
And rid me of the Pain.

**MONESES**
For only Death,
And the last Night can shut out my Arpasia.

[The **MUTES** strangle **MONESES**.

**ARPASIA**
Oh! dismal! 'tis not to be born. Ye Moralists,
Ye Talkers, what are all your Precepts now?
Patience? Distraction? blast the Tyrant, blast him!
Avenging Lightnings, snatch him hence, ye Fiends!
Love! Death! Moneses! Nature can no more,
Ruin is on her, and she sinks at once.

[She sinks down.

**BAJAZET**
Help, Haly, raise her up, and bear her out.

**HALY**
Alas! she saints.

**ARPASIA**
No, Tyrant, 'tis in vain;
Oh! I am now beyond thy cruel Pow'r:
The Peaceful Slumber of the Grave is on me;
Ev'n all the tedious Day of Life I've wander'd,
Bewild r'd with Misfortunes;
At length 'tis Night, and I have reach'd my home:
Forg tting all the Toils and Troubles past,
Weary I'll lay me down, and sleep till—Oh!

[She dies.

**BAJAZET**
Fly, ye Slaves,
And fetch me Cordials. No she shall not die.
Spight of her sullen Pride, I'll hold in Life,
And force her to be blest against her Will

**HALY**
Already 'tis beyond the Power of Art;
For see a deadly Cold has froze the Blood,
The pliant Limbs grow stiff, and lose their use,
And all the animating Fire is quench'd;
Ev'n Beauty too is dead; an ashy Pale
Grows o'er the Roses, the red Lips have lost
Their flagrant Hew, for want of that sweet Breath
That blest 'em with its Odours as it past.

**BAJAZET**

Can it be possible? Can Rage and Grief,
Can Love and Indignation be so fierce,
So mortal in a Woman's Heart? Confusion!
Is she escap'd then? What is Royalty?
If those, that are my Slaves, and should live for me,
Can die, and bid Defiance to my Power.

[Enter the **DERVISE**.

**DERVISE**
The valiant Omar sends, to tell thy Greatness,
The Hour of Flight is come, and urges haste,
Since he descries near Tamerlane's Pavilion,
Bright Troops of crowding Torches, who from thence
On either Hand stretch far into the Night,
And seem to form a shining Front of Battle.
Behold, ev'n from this place, thou may'st discern 'em.

[Looking out.

**BAJAZET**
By Alha! yes! they cast a Day around 'em,
And the Plain seems thick set with Stars, as Heav'n.
Ha! or my Eyes are false, they move this way.
'Tis certain so. Fly, Haly, to our Daughter.

[Exit **HALY**.

Let some secure the Christian Prince Axalla;
We will be gone this Minute.

[Enter **OMAR**.

**OMAR**
Lost! Undone!

**BAJAZET**
What mean'st thou?

**OMAR**
All our hopes of Flight are lost,
Mirvan and Zama, with the Parthian Horse,
Enclose us round, they hold us in a Toil.

**BAJAZET**
Ha! whence this unexpected Curse of Chance?

**OMAR**

Too late I learnt, that early in the Night
A Slave was suffer'd by the Princess Order,
Chast Virgins, tender Wives, and pious Matrons;
Ye holy Martyrs, who, with wond'rous Faith,
And Constancy unshaken, have sustain'd
The Rage of cruel Men, and fiery Persecution;
Come to my Aid, and teach me to defie
The Malice of this Fiend. I feel, I feel
Your sacred Spirit arm me to Resistance.
Yes, Tyrant, I will stand this shock of Fate;
Will live to triumph o'er them, for a Moment;
Then die well pleas'd, and follow my Moneses.

**BAJAZET**
Thou talk'st it well: But talking is thy Privilege,
'Tis all the boasted Courage of thy Sex;
Tho', for thy Soul, thou dar'st not meet the Danger.

**ARPASIA**
By all my hops of Happiness! I dare—
My Soul is come within her ken of Heav'n;
Charm'd with the Joys and Beauties of that place,
Her Thoughts, and all her Cares she fixes there,
And 'tis in vain for thee, to rage below:
Thus Stars shine bright, and keep their place above,
Tho' ruffling Winds deform this lower World.

**BAJAZET**
This Moment is the Trial.

**ARPASIA**
Let it come;
This Moment then shall shew I am a Greek,
And speak my Country's Courage in my suff'ring.

**BAJAZET**
Here, Mercy, I disclaim thee, mark me, Traitress!
My Love prepares a Victim to thy Pride,
And when it greets thee next, 'twill be in Blood.

[Exit **BAJAZET**.

**ARPASIA**
My Heart beats higher, and my nimble Spirits
Ride swiftly thro' their purple Channels round:
'Tis the last blaze of Life: Nature revives
Like a dim winking Lamp, that slashes brightly
With parting Light, and strait is Dark for ever.

And see! my last of Sorrows is at Hand:
Death and Moneses come together to me;
As if my Stars that had so long been cruel,
Grew kind at last, and gave me all I wish.

[Enter **MONESES**, guarded by some **MUTES**, **OTHERS** attending with a Cup of Poison and a Bow-string.

**MONESES**
I charge ye, ye Ministers of Fate,
Be swift to execute your Master's Will,
Bear me to my Arpasia; let me tell her,
The Tyrant is grown kind. He bids me go,
And die beneath her Feet. A Joy shoots thro'
My drooping Breast, as often, when the Trumpet
Has call'd my youthful Ardour forth to Battle;
High in my Hopes, and ravisht with the Sound,
I have rush'd eager on amidst the foremost
To purchase Victory, or glorious Death.

**ARPASIA**
If it be Happiness, alas! to die,
To lye forgotten in the silent Grave,
To Love, and Glory lost, and from among
The great Creator's Works expung'd and blotted,
Then very shortly shall we both be happy.

**MONESES**
There is no room for Doubt, 'tis certain Bliss;
The Tyrant's cruel Violence, thy Loss,
Already seem more light, nor has my Soul,
One unrepented Guilt upon remembrance,
To make me dread the Justice of hereafter;
But standing now on the last Verge of Life,
Boldly I view the vast Abyss, Eternity,
Eager to plunge, and leave my Woes behind me.

**ARPASIA**
By all the Truth of our past Lives I vow!
To die! appears a very nothing to me:
But oh! Moneses, should I not allow
Somewhat to Love, and to my Sexes tenderness,
This very Now, I could put off my Being,
Without a Groan; but to behold thee die—
Nature shrinks in me, at the dreadful Thought,
Nor can my Constancy sustain this Blow.

**MONESES**
Since thou art arm'd for all things, after Death.

Why should the Pomp and Preparation of it
Be frightful to thy Eyes? There's not a Pain,
Which Age, or Sickness brings, the least Disorder,
That vexes any part of this fine Frame,
Is full as grievous: All that the Mind feels
Is much, much more.—And see, I go to prove it.

[Enter a **MUTE**; he signs to the rest, who proffer the Bow-string to **MONESES**.

**ARPASIA**
Think e'er we part!

**MONESES**
Of what?
To pass the Guard; I clove the Villain down,
Who yielded to his Flight; but that's poor Vengeance.
That Fugitive has rais'd the Camp upon us,
And unperceiv'd by favour of the Night,
In silence they have marcht to intercept us.

**BAJAZET**
My Daughter! oh! the Traitress!

**DERVISE**
Yet, we have
Axalla in our Power, and angry Tamerlane
Will buy his Favourite's Life, on any Terms.

**OMAR**
With these few Friends I have, I for a while,
Can face their Force; if they refuse us Peace,
Revenge shall sweeten Ruin, and 'twill Joy me,
To drag my Foe down with me, in my Fall.

[Exit **OMAR**.

[Enter **HALY**, with **SELIMA** weeping.

**BAJAZET**
See where she comes! with well-dissembled Innocence,
With Truth, and Faith so lovely in her Face,
As if she durst ev'n disavow the Falshood.—
Hop'st thou to make amends with trifling Tears,
For my lost Crown, and disappointed Vengeance?
Ungrateful Selima! thy Father's Curse!
Bring forth the Minion of her foolish Heart;
He dies this Moment.—

**HALY**
Would I could not speak
The Crime of fatal Love, the Slave who fled,
By whom we are undone; was that Axalla.

**BAJAZET**
Ha! say'st thou?—

**HALY**
Hid beneath that vile Appearance,
The Princess found a means for his Escape.

**SELIMA**
I am undone! ev'n Nature has disclaim'd me;
My Father! have I lost you all?—My Father!

**BAJAZET**
Talk'st thou of Nature? who hast broke her Bands!
Thou art my Bane, thou Witch! thou Infant Parricide!
But I will study to be strangely cruel,
I will forget the Folly of my Fondness.
Drive all the Father from my Breast, now snatch thee,
Tear thee to pieces, drink thy treacherous Blood,
And make thee answer all my great Revenge:
Now, now, thou Traitress!

[Offers to kill her.

**SELIMA**
Plunge the Poniard deep!

[She embraces him.

The Life my Father gave shall hear his Summons,
And issue at the Wound—Start not, to feel
My Heart's warm Blood gush out upon your Hands,
Since from your Spring I drew the Purple Stream,
And I must pay it back, if you demand it.

**BAJAZET**
Hence! from my Thoughts! thou soft relenting Weakness.
Hast thou not giv'n me up a Prey? betray'd me?

**SELIMA**
Oh! not for Worlds, not ev'n for all the Joys
Love, or the Prophet's Paradise can give;
Amidst the Fears, and Sorrows of my Soul,
Amidst the thousand Pains of anxious Tenderness,

I made the gentle kind Axalla swear,
Your Life, your Crown, and Honour should be safe.

**BAJAZET**
Away! my Soul disdains the vile Dependance.
No, let me rather die, die like a King:
Shall I fall down at the proud Tartar's Foot?
And say, Have Mercy on me? Hark, they come.

[Shout.

Disgrace will overtake my lingring Hand:
Die then, thy Father's Shame, and thine, die with thee.

[Offers to kill her.

**SELIMA**
For Heaven, for Pity's sake.

**BAJAZET**
No more, thou Trifler!

[She catches hold of his Arm.

Ha! dar'st thou bar my Will? Tear off her Hold.

**SELIMA**
What not for Life? Shou'd I not plead for Life?
When Nature teaches ev'n the brute Creation,
To hold fast that, her best, her noblest Gift.
Look on my Eyes, whom you so oft have kist,
And swore, they were your best lov'd Queen's, my Mothers.
Behold 'em now streaming for Mercy, Mercy!
Look on me, and deny me, if you can;
'Tis but for Life I beg, is that a Boon
So hard for me t' obtain? or you to grant?
Oh! spare me! spare your Selima, my Father.

**BAJAZET**
A lazy Sloth hangs on my Resolution;
It is my Selima!—Ha! What? my Child?
And can I murder her?—Dreadful Imagination!
Again they come. I leave her to my Foes!

[Shout.

And shall they triumph o'er the Race of Bajazet?
Die Selima! Is that a Father's Voice?

Rouse, rouse my Fury! yes she dies, the Victim
To my lost hopes. Out! out! thou foolish Nature!
Justly she shares the Ruin she has made,
Seize her,

[To the **MUTES**.

—ye Slaves, and strangle her this moment.

**SELIMA**
Oh! let me die by you! Behold my Breast!
I wo'not shrink; oh! save me but from these.

[The **MUTES** seize her.

**BAJAZET**
Dispatch.

**SELIMA**
But for a moment, while I pray,
That Heav'n may guard my Royal Father.

**BAJAZET**
Dogs!

**SELIMA**
That you may only bless me, e'er I die.

[Shout.

**BAJAZET**
Ye tedious Villains! then the Work is mine.

[As **BAJAZET** runs at **SELIMA** with his Sword, Enter **TAMERLANE**, **AXALLA**, &c. **AXALLA** gets between
**BAJAZET** and **SELIMA**, whilst **TAMERLANE** and the rest drive **BAJAZET** and the **MUTES** off the Stage.

**AXALLA**
And am I come to save thee? Oh! my Joy!
Be this the whitest Hour of all my Life;
This one Success is more, than all my Wars,
The noblest, dearest Glory of my Sword.

**SELIMA**
Alas, Axalla, Death has been around me,
My Coward Soul still trembles at the Fright,
And seems but half secure, ev'n in thy Arms.

**AXALLA**

Retire, my Fair, and let me guard thee forth;
Blood and tumultuous Slaughter are about us,
And Danger in her ugliest Forms is here;
Nor will the pleasure of my Heart be full,
'Till all my Fears are ended in thy Safety.

[Exeunt **AXALLA**, and **SELIMA**.

[Enter **TAMERLANE**, the **PRINCE of TANAIS**, **ZAMA**, **MIRVAN**, and **SOLDIERS**; with **BAJAZET**, **OMAR**, and the **DERVISE**, Prisoners.

**TAMERLANE**
Morcy at length gives up her peaceful Scepter,
And Justice sternly takes her turn to govern;
'Tis a rank World, and asks her keenest Sword,
To cut up Villany of monstrous growth.
Zama, take care, that with the earliest dawn,
Those Traitors meet the Fate, their Treason merits.

[Pointing to **OMAR** and the **DERVISE**.

[To **BAJAZET**.
For thee, thou Tyrant, whose oppressive Violence
Has ruin'd those, thou should'st protect at home,
Whose Wars, whose Slaughters, whose Assassinations,
(That basest thirst of Blood, that sin of Cowards)
Whose Faith so often giv'n, and always violated,
Have been th' Offence of Heav'n, and Plague of Earth,
What Punishment is equal to thy Crimes?
The Doom, thy Rage design'd for me, be thine:
Clos'd in a Cage, like some destructive Beast,
I'll have thee born about, in publick View,
A great Example of that Righteous Vengeance
That waits on Cruelty, and Pride like thine.

**BAJAZET**
It is beneath me, to decline my Fate:
I stand prepar'd to meet thy utmost Hate:
Yet think not, I will long thy Triumph see,
None want the means, when the Soul dares be free;
I'll Curse thee with my last, my parting Breath,
And keep the Courage of my Life in Death;
Then boldly venture on that World unknown,
It cannot use me worse, than this has done.

[Exit **BAJAZET** guarded.

**TAMERLANE**

Behold the vain Effects of Earth-born Pride,
That scorn'd Heav'n's Laws, and all its Pow'r defy'd;
That could the Hand, which form'd it first, forget,
And fondly say, I made my self, be great:
And justly those above assert their Sway,
And teach ev'n Kings what Homage they should pay
And then Rule best, when mindful to Obey.

[Exeunt.


## EPILOGUE

Spoke by **MRS BRACEGIRDLE**

Too well we saw what must have been our Fate,
When Harmony with Beauty join'd of late,
Threaten'd the Ruin of our sinking State;
'Till you, from whom our Being we receive,
In pity bid your own Creation live.
With moving Sounds you kindly drew the Fair,
And fix'd, once more, that shining Circle here.
The Lyre you bring is half Apollo's Praise;
Be ours the Task to win and wear his Bays.
Thin Houses were before so frequent to us,
We wanted not a Project to undo us.
We seldom saw your Honours but by chance,
As some Folks meet their Friends of Spain and France
'Twas Verse decay'd, or Politicks improv'd,
That had estrang'd you thus from what you lov'd.
Time was, when busie Faces were a Jest,
When Wit and Pleasure were in most request;
When chearful Theaters with Crowds were grac'd
But those good Days of Poetry are past:
Now [.....] an empty Pit,
[.....] a Lecture, sit,
[.....] take Notes and[.....] Evidence 'gainst
Those [.....]
[.....] Peace and [.....]
With careful [.....] at Tom's and Will's they [.....]
And ask, who did Elections lose or get
Our Friend has lost it—Faith I'm sorry for't
He's a good Man, and ne'er was for the Court
He to no Government will sue for Grace;
By want of Merit, safe against a Place:
By spight a Patriot made, and sworn t'oppose
All who are uppermost, as England's Foes.

Let Whig or Tory, any side prevail,
Still 'tis his constant Privilege to rail.
Another, that the Tax and War may cease,
Talks of the Duke of Anjou's Right, and Peace;
And, from Spain's wise Example, is for taking
A Vice-Roy of the mighty Monarch's making;
Who should all Rights and Liberties maintain,
And English Laws by learn'd Dragoons explain.
Come, leave these Politicks, and follow Wit;
Here uncontroll'd you may in Judgment sit,
We'll never differ with a crowded Pit.
We'll take you all, ev'n on your own Conditions,
Think you Great Men, and wond'rous Politicians.
And if you slight the Offers which we make you,
No Brentford Princes will for Statesmen take you

Nicholas Rowe – A Concise Bibliography

## Poems
A Poem upon the Late Glorious Successes of Her Majesty's Arms (1707)
Poems on Several Occasions (1714)
Maecenas. Verses occasion'd by the honours conferr'd on the Right Honourable Earl of Halifax (1714)
Ode for the New Year MDCCXVI (1716)

## Original Plays
The Ambitious Stepmother (1700)
Tamerlane (1702)
The Biter (1705)
Ulysses (1705)
The Royal Convert (1707)
The Tragedy of Jane Shore (1714)
Lady Jane Grey (1715)

## Adaptations and Translations
The Fair Penitent (1702/3), an adaptation of Massinger and Field's The Fatal Dowry
Lucan (1718), a paraphrase of the Pharsalia
Callipaedia (date unknown), translation of Claude Quillet

## Edited Works
The Works of William Shakespear (London: 1709), first modern edition of the plays.

## Miscellaneous Works
Memoir of Boileau (date unknown), prefixed to translation of Lutrin
Some Account of the Life of Mr. William Shakespear

www.ingramcontent.com/pod-product-compliance
Lightning Source LLC
Chambersburg PA
CBHW021938040426
42448CB00008B/1136